ESL/ELL TEACHER'S GUIDE

PACEMAKER®

World History

GLOBE FEARON
Pearson Learning Group

The following people have contributed to the development of this product:
Art and Design: Tricia Battipede, Robert Dobaczewski, Joan Jacobus
Editorial: Monica Glina
Manufacturing: Michele Uhl
Marketing: Clare Harrison, Anna Mazzoccoli
Production: Carlos Blas, Meredith Tenety
Publishing Operations: Jennifer Van Der Heide

Reviewers

Sheila D. Acevedo, ESOL Manager for Alternative Education,
Palm Beach School District, Palm Beach, FL

Ann Hilborn, former ESL/ELL teacher, coordinator, and curriculum writer for the
Houston Independent School District; currently an ESL/ELL consultant in Texas

Barbara Ishida, Bilingual Language Development Specialist,
Modesto City Schools, Modesto, CA

Linda D. Larson, ESOL Resource Teacher/Coordinator,
School Board of Palm Beach County, Royal Palm Beach, FL

Maribel Nieves, ESL/ELL Teacher, Martin Luther King, Jr. High School, New York, NY

Sandra Prez, Bilingual Coordinator, District 116, Round Lake, IL

Joseph Sklar, Instructional Facilitator, Oakland Unified School District, Oakland, CA

Cover: All photos © Pearson Learning Group unless otherwise noted.
African Waist Pendant: © 2000, Waist pendant representing Idia, mother of Oba Esigie, part of ceremonial costume, Benin, 16th Century/The Bridgeman Art Library. Astronaut: Stone/Getty Images. Sphinx: Stone/Getty Images. Astrolabe: The Granger Collection, New York. Decorative Box from Russia: Dorling Kindersley. Fan: Dorling Kindersley. Aztec Calendar: National Museum of Anthropology, Mexico City/Michael Zabe/Art Resource, NY.

Copyright © 2003 by Pearson Education, Inc., publishing as Globe Fearon®, an imprint of Pearson Learning Group, 299 Jefferson Road, Parsippany, NJ 07054. All rights reserved. No part of this book may be reproduced or transmitted in any form or by any means, electronic, or mechanical, including photocopying, recording, or by any information storage and retrieval system, without permission in writing from the publisher, except for Pages 72-84, which may be reproduced for classroom use only. For information regarding permission(s), write to Rights and Permissions Department.

Globe Fearon® is a registered trademark of Globe Fearon, Inc.
Pacemaker® is a registered trademark of Pearson Education, Inc.

ISBN 0-13-024004-4
Printed in the United States of America
 2 3 4 5 6 7 8 9 10   06 05 04

1-800-321-3106
www.pearsonlearning.com

Contents

Teaching ESL/ELL in the Classroom iv
The Pacemaker® Curriculum iv
How Do I Use the *Pacemaker® ESL/ELL Guide*? v
Selecting the Appropriate Leveled Questions viii
Effective Strategies for ESL/ELL Students ix
Previewing Strategies xii
Vocabulary Strategies xiii

UNIT 1 LOOKING AT THE WORLD'S HISTORY

| Chapter 1 | What Is History? .... 2 |
| Chapter 2 | Early Humans: The Story Begins ...... 4 |

UNIT 2 ANCIENT CIVILIZATIONS

Chapter 3	Sumerians: The First Great Civilization 6
Chapter 4	Ancient Egypt: Land of the Pharaohs 8
Chapter 5	Mediterranean Kingdoms 10
Chapter 6	Early Civilizations of India, China, and the Americas 12

UNIT 3 THE ORIGINS OF WESTERN CIVILIZATION: GREECE AND ROME

Chapter 7	Greek City-States and the Golden Age 14
Chapter 8	Alexander the Great 16
Chapter 9	The Rise of Rome 18

UNIT 4 THE MIDDLE AGES

Chapter 10	The Barbarians and the Vikings 20
Chapter 11	The Lords and the Serfs 22
Chapter 12	Islam and the Crusades 24

UNIT 5 THE RENAISSANCE

| Chapter 13 | New Ideas: The Renaissance .... 26 |
| Chapter 14 | Kings and Queens .... 28 |

UNIT 6 THE AGE OF EXPLORATION AND CONQUEST

| Chapter 15 | To the East; To the West .... 30 |
| Chapter 16 | Explorers, Traders, and Settlers ...... 32 |

UNIT 7 THE BIRTH OF DEMOCRACY

| Chapter 17 | The Struggle for Democracy .... 34 |
| Chapter 18 | Revolution in France .... 36 |

UNIT 8 THE AGE OF IMPERIALISM

Chapter 19	The Industrial Revolution 38
Chapter 20	Independence in Latin America 40
Chapter 21	The United States Gains Power 42
Chapter 22	Imperialism and the Far East 44
Chapter 23	Imperialism and India 46
Chapter 24	Imperialism and Africa 48

UNIT 9 NATIONALISM AND THE SPREAD OF WAR AND REVOLUTION

Chapter 25	The Unifications of Italy and Germany 50
Chapter 26	World War I 52
Chapter 27	Revolution in Russia: The Birth of the Soviet Union 54
Chapter 28	World War II 56

UNIT 10 THE POSTWAR WORLD

Chapter 29	Changes in Europe 58
Chapter 30	Changes in Asia and Africa 60
Chapter 31	The Middle East 62
Chapter 32	The Death of the Soviet Union 64
Chapter 33	Latin America After World War II ... 66
Chapter 34	The World Today 68

GRAPHIC ORGANIZERS

About the Graphic Organizers 70
Who, What, Why, Where, When, and How Chart 72
Spider Web 73
Venn Diagram 74
Timeline 75
Outline 76
Sequence of Events Chart 77
Description Web 78
KWL Chart 79
Four-column Chart 80
Idea Web 81
Individual Activity Rubric 82
Group Activity Rubric 83
Chapter Goals and Self-assessment 84

Teaching ESL/ELL in the Classroom

As cross-cultural mobility increases, teachers are mindful of their responsibility in the preparation of global citizens. All classrooms are becoming ESL/ELL classrooms, and many teachers are confronting new instructional challenges as demographics shift and diversity multiplies.

On the one hand, there is concern for meeting the needs of students who bring issues and challenges that teachers often feel underprepared to meet. On the other, there is renewal and excitement as teachers and students open to the perspectives of other cultures, and classrooms assume an international orientation.

Helping the ESL/ELL learner to succeed in the academic classroom has required all educators to rethink their roles as teacher, to search for new instructional tools, and to become simultaneously a language teacher, reading teacher, and academic content teacher. To help teachers meet this formidable task, both students and teachers must have teaching and learning resources that make academic content accessible.

The Pacemaker® Curriculum

Typically, schools adopt one of two structures for academic classes: sheltered content or regular mainstream. The Pacemaker® curriculum is perfectly suited for either of those environments. Designed for students who read independently at a 3.0 to 4.0 reading level, a Pacemaker® text normally corresponds to a student at mid-intermediate level of language proficiency. This is the level when most ESL/ELL students are required to deal with the cognitively demanding language of academic content classes.

When students are given sheltered content instruction, the Pacemaker® curriculum is an ideal classroom text for intermediate and advanced level students.

In schools where sheltered content classes are unavailable, Pacemaker® can be a valuable text or resource for ESL/ELL students in the regular content classroom because it provides information in small manageable sections at a level that students can comprehend.

When Pacemaker® materials are provided in place of, or in addition to, the standard text, students can access academic content rather than struggle with a grade-level text that is beyond their current language proficiency. Although language skills of ESL/ELL students are in a developmental stage, they can be held to the same high standards of critical inquiry as their on-level classmates when input is comprehensible. The Pacemaker® curriculum is also an ideal tool that can be used to preview and review by preparing students for and enhancing their comprehension of the content they will be accessing in their grade-level tests.

Because the Pacemaker® materials are within the expected reading levels of a second-language learner and the content is presented in manageable sections, ESL/ELL students are encouraged and enabled to be active participants rather than silent observers in the academic classroom.

How Do I Use the *Pacemaker® ESL/ELL Guide* in My Classroom?

Teaching academic content requires attention to both information and skills. While content teachers are not reading teachers, time spent previewing and engaging in prestudy activities provides an opportunity to teach valuable skills that will serve students in all areas of studies. For ESL/ELL students, time spent in previewing will assure greater comprehension and retention. It will prepare them not only for reading, but also for participation in class discussions, collaborative work, and individual or group projects.

The following suggestions are easily managed in a sheltered content class. If the class is a regular-content class, ESL/ELL students can be provided with a Pacemaker® text while others use a grade-level text. If an aide is not available to work with ESL/ELL students and the teacher must work with both groups, it is not necessary to divide the class and teach two separate groups. Using the high-interest Pacemaker® texts for ESL/ELL students makes it possible to integrate two different texts under unifying objectives. The abundance of resources in the Pacemaker® curriculum to support instruction makes it possible to provide alternate materials with minimum effort.

Each chapter of the Pacemaker® Student Edition is supported by a two-page lesson plan, which follows an Into-Through-Beyond model. The lesson plan begins by introducing students to the chapter content, or bringing them into the content. It then helps students work through the content they have acquired by engaging in relevant activities. Finally, it takes students beyond what they have learned by assessing what they learned and affording them an opportunity to summarize the important points of the chapter.

 ## Introducing the Chapter

This section is made up of two parts: Tapping Prior Knowledge and Preteaching Vocabulary.

Tapping Prior Knowledge

All students, and ESL/ELL students in particular, improve comprehension when they can connect what they already know to the subject. Focusing on the colorful artwork, the title, a caption, a subheading, or a Pacemaker® feature will help students to make important initial connections.

Tapping Prior Knowledge gives students the opportunity to

- preview the chapter.
- access their prior knowledge about a topic.
- think about an overarching question that connects students prior knowledge to chapter content.

Preteaching Vocabulary

Preteaching Vocabulary offers students an opportunity to:

- identify and define words and phrases that are unfamiliar to them. You may wish to ask students to keep a Word Log in which they can list the words and phrases that they identify for Personalizing Vocabulary. This is also an opportunity for students to learn the proper pronunciation of the vocabulary words and phrases. When reviewing the pronunciation of the vocabulary words and phrases with your students, you may wish to pronounce them and have students listen to the pronunciation; pronounce them and ask your students to repeat each one; or pronounce them and have your students repeat them in a choral read. You may wish to provide a phonetic spelling for students to use in addition to the strategies mentioned above.

- engage in a variety of activities across chapters that are based on specific, academic content words and phrases that are integral to their understanding of the subject matter, as well as words and phrases that are challenging for ESL/ELL students, such as double-meaning words and phrases and idiomatic expressions.

▶ Learning Objectives

All learners need concrete and concise explanations of what they will be expected to learn. Every Pacemaker® outlines specific Learning Objectives for each chapter. Reading those objectives with your students as they begin the chapter connects them all to the same goals, guides the lesson, and helps prepare students for future assessment.

Turn to the end of the chapter and have students work in pairs or small groups to connect Learning Objectives to the Chapter Review. Good students use questions in the text to guide them in reading and understanding. ESL/ELL students need to be directed to these tools and shown how the tools can help them to understand what they are reading and studying. This will reinforce what students are expected to learn and help to guide their reading. You may also wish to distribute the Chapter Goals and Self-assessment on page 84 of this guide and have students write the list of objectives that they are expected to master by the end of the chapter. This will allow students to evaluate their own achievement of learning goals.

▶ Applying Content Knowledge

All students improve comprehension when they are able to apply what they have learned. Activities that incorporate the use of graphic organizers as well as activities that allow students to (re)address chapter content help cultivate the initial connections they made in Tapping Prior Knowledge.

Each activity in Applying Content Knowledge:

- uses Specifically Designed Academic Instruction in English strategies. SDAIE strategies focus on delivering grade-level content and covering grade-level standards in a way that is personally relevant for and comprehensible to the student.

- uses the Cognitive Academic Language Learning Approach. CALLA is designed to help ESL/ELL students succeed academically by addressing topics from the major content subjects, developing academic language skills, and offering explicit instruction on learning strategies.
- offers activities that enhance students' content knowledge through reading, writing, speaking, and listening.
- allows students to use a variety of graphic organizers. Several organizers are provided on pages 70–84 of this guide. Using them will not only help students to understand what they read, it will also teach them the variety of ways material is organized.

▶ Assessing Content Knowledge

This section provides three levels of questions tailored to beginning ESL/ELL students, intermediate ESL/ELL students, and advanced ESL/ELL students. [See page viii of this guide for placement criteria.] Questions can be answered orally or in writing. This section also provides teachers' annotations at point of use.

As an alternative, the leveled questions can also be used for discussion. If the questions are used for discussion, allow ESL/ELL students adequate time to process the question by using a cooperative strategy like putting students in small groups made up of students with varied language abilities. Pose the question and then allow the group to process the answer so that each group member can respond. Then, allow one member of each group to give an answer. This strategy is also ideal for reviewing chapter content.

Beginning Level Students
- Specific page references are provided to scaffold beginning ESL/ELL students.
- Beginning ESL/ELL students are asked to respond to questions using short verbal responses.

Intermediate Level Students
- More general skill or section references are provided to scaffold intermediate ESL/ELL students.
- Intermediate ESL/ELL students are asked to respond to questions using verbal responses or short written responses.

Advanced Level Students
- Since advanced students are expected to be able to answer the questions in the Chapter Review at the end of each chapter in the Student Edition, no page or skill/section references are provided for the advanced ESL/ELL students.
- Advanced ESL/ELL students are asked to respond to questions in complete written sentences.

▶ Closing the Chapter

Closing the Chapter provides an opportunity for students to assess the key points of the chapter and summarize them. Students are frequently asked to write a summary about what they learned, but you may wish to ask beginning ESL/ELL students to give an oral report of what they learned.

Selecting the Appropriate Leveled Questions

This guide includes three levels of questions to address the different levels of students' language proficiency.

Since there are students who can speak English but have difficulty reading it, the leveled questions presented in this guide should be chosen for a student based on the student's level of reading proficiency. The following criteria are based on student competencies at the beginning of the year, which are expected to increase during the course of the academic year. The three levels of questions provided in each lesson plan of this guide are also available as reproducible pages that can be downloaded from www.esl-ell.com. Level A corresponds to the Beginning Level Questions; Level B corresponds to the Intermediate Level Questions; and Level C corresponds to the Advanced Level Questions.

▶ Beginning Level Questions – Level A

Beginning Level Students:

- range from having no comprehension to the ability to read and comprehend simple sentences in present continuous or simple present tense.
- are able to answer straightforward comprehension questions (*who*, *what*, *when*, *where*) that require only simple responses.
- are able to write paragraphs of one to five lines.
- are able to read and write at a kindergarten to a first-grade level.
- should be able to complete the Beginning Level Questions in this guide.

▶ Intermediate Level Questions – Level B

Intermediate Level Students:

- satisfy all of the beginning level criteria.
- are able to read and comprehend simple past and future tense sentences.
- are able to answer comprehension questions that also include *how* and *why* with more complex responses.
- are able to write a well-developed paragraph.
- are able to read and write from a second- to a fourth-grade level.
- should be able to complete the Intermediate Level Questions in this guide.

▶ Advanced Level Questions – Level C

Advanced Level Students:

- satisfy all of the beginning and intermediate level criteria.
- are able to read and comprehend more complex sentence constructions.
- are able to use past and some perfect tense constructions in their writing.
- are able to respond to questions that require inference and conclusions.
- are able to write multi-paragraph compositions.
- are able to read and write at a level that can extend from third to fifth grade.
- should be able to complete the questions in the Chapter Review in the Student Edition as well as the Advanced Level Questions in this guide.

Effective Strategies for ESL/ELL Students

While the *Pacemaker® ESL/ELL Guide* is designed to help teachers of ESL/ELL students help their students access content knowledge, there are some additional strategies that are centered around the motivation of and effective study skills for ESL/ELL students.

Classroom Techniques

Encourage risk-taking by keeping a low-anxiety environment.

- Strive for genuine communication with students. Students' fears are calmed when teachers share information about themselves and invite students to talk about themselves and their experiences.
- Provide game-like activities.
- Adjust speech. Speak a little more slowly and distinctly.
- Share information across cultures.
- Provide materials that support comprehension.
- Practice a little of the students' languages.

Provide academic scaffolds to help your students access the content.

- Model all activities for your students. Provide examples and writing models.
- Give students a topic outline for note-taking.
- Encourage students to use previewing strategies, while-reading strategies, and post-reading strategies.
- Provide study questions and guides.
- Identify organizational cues, such as titles, subtitles, and charts.
- Afford students longer reading time, as well as extended time for assignments and test completion.

Building Language Skills

Read to students. By reading short passages in answer to a question or as an introduction, ESL/ELL students receive the added benefit of hearing academic language, cadence, rhythm, and pronunciation.

When reading from a source other than the Student Edition, provide handouts or use an overhead, so students can see and hear the information.

Teach students to read academic material several times. As academic learners, we all expect to read a selection, a page, a chapter, or a section more than once. Encourage students to:

- survey an academic assignment once for general information and vocabulary.
- organize reading into smaller chunks for understanding.
- read a third time for higher-level critical thinking skills.

In-class reading time is usually no more than 10 to 15 minutes. Regular classroom students may be expected to read more material in that time frame, but they need not read for a longer period of time. If longer reading assignments are desired for homework, reading can be previewed in advance of any assignment and graphic organizers provided to help guide ESL/ELL students' reading.

Maximize language output. While students should be given opportunities to interact without depending heavily on language, the more practical opportunities students have to speak and write, the more proficient they will become. These opportunities may begin with communication of their own life experiences and world knowledge.

Provide open-ended writing assignments and opportunities for ESL/ELL students to express their thoughts and feelings. Some of these include:

- journals.
- descriptions of experiences or feelings.
- response to art, photos, and audio-visuals.

The Tapping Prior Knowledge section, which highlights the art and photos in each chapter and often asks students to relate the content to their own experiences, is an ideal opportunity for students to express their thoughts and feelings. For example, you may wish to ask students to keep a journal and record their initial responses to the visual image(s) that appear(s) on the first page of each chapter. You may also consider having students choose to describe a visual image that appears in the chapter.

Complete activities with a writing assignment. ESL/ELL students may need adjustments to the writing assignments, such as:

- shorter writing assignments.
- more time to complete writing.
- frequent opportunities to work with peers in revising and editing.

Occasionally it will be necessary to assign a different topic. *The Pacemaker® ESL/ELL Guide* provides writing opportunities in conjunction with many of the activities that help students reinforce chapter content.

Learning Strategies

Provide opportunities for different groups to work together, share information, and be a resource for each other.

Provide opportunities for students to interact without depending heavily on language. Students can work to access content knowledge by:

- doing projects and making posters, pictures, and collages.
- using manipulatives.
- using charts.
- using numbered lists, bulleted lists, graphs, tables, and models.
- role-playing.

Use visuals, pictures, realia, video clips, and actions to teach vocabulary and to make concepts concrete and understandable. Maps, play money, artwork, globes, and pictures are effective, tangible ways to help students access content.

Use graphic organizers for note-taking, organizing information, and writing. Diagrams and charts are an effective way to teach students to organize information and visualize patterns and structures. Graphic organizers can be downloaded from www.esl-ell.com.

Customizing Student Assessment

Assess your students' successes by focusing on the "big picture."

- Grade a combination of process and product.
- Recognize effort and improvement in ways other than grades.
- Allow rewrites and test corrections to improve grades and understanding.
- Congratulate students on small successes.
- Focus on meaning and content knowledge, not grammar mistakes, in students' written work.
- Use alternative assessments, such as performance-based assessments, self-ratings, projects, and portfolios.
- Adjust your grading scale where appropriate.

At Home

Help students manage their own success. Reinforce the importance of organizing homework, academic tasks, and extracurricular activities using a calendar like the one shown below.

Monday	Tuesday	Wednesday	Thursday	Friday
soccer practice 3:00-5:30	study time 5:00-6:00	soccer practice 3:00-5:30	study time 5:00-6:00	
dinner 6:00-7:00	dinner 6:00-7:00	dinner 6:00-7:00	dinner 6:00-7:00	dinner 6:00-7:00
study time 7:00-8:00	orchestra 7:30-9:00		climbing club 8:00-9:00	

You may wish to work with students to schedule activities from this guide that you assign as homework. Homework gives parents and caregivers an opportunity to be involved with their students.

Ann Hilborn

Ann Hilborn, a former ESL/ELL teacher, coordinator, and curriculum writer for the Houston Independent School District, is currently an ESL/ELL consultant in Texas.

Previewing Strategies

When students preview, they set a purpose for reading, they think about what they already know about a topic, and they get a general idea of what they will learn. Activities that students engage in before reading help them prepare to learn new information. Previewing helps students incorporate what they read into their existing knowledge. During previewing, students should identify key terms, assess the level of difficulty and length of what they will be reading, gain a general sense of the topic and major subtopics, understand text organization, and determine how this information relates to what they already know.

▶ Create a Plan for Reading.

This task requires students to think about why they are reading. *What was the purpose of the assignment?* If students are unclear about the answer to this question, they need to find out why they are reading. Next, students should look at the assignment to get a sense of how difficult it is. *Can they read the assignment in one session, or should they break it into several sessions?*

▶ Think About What They Know About the Topic.

Students who engage with the text create a scaffold for learning. When they bring prior knowledge to bear on their readings, students become involved with the text.

▶ Preview the Selection.

When students preview, they think about what they already know about a topic and get a general idea of what they will learn. Students should:

- look at the title and subheadings. These signal important ideas and usually hint at text organization.

- look at other visual aids. These include words within the text in italic or bold type, which may be vocabulary words or new concepts. Students should also look at aids, such as maps, photos, charts, illustrations, numbered lists, and bulleted lists. This will give ESL/ELL students more contextual information to aid with comprehension.

- read the first and last paragraphs. These often contain the thesis or major points of the reading. Remind students to connect what they are previewing with what they already know about the topic.

- read the first sentence or topic sentence of each paragraph. Often, the main point of a paragraph is found at the beginning.

- get an idea of the text structure. If students understand how the text is organized—for example, chronologically or in cause-and-effect form—they will be better able to follow the text.

Vocabulary Strategies

Each two-page lesson plan provides a vocabulary activity for its chapter. While the vocabulary activities in this guide support the chapters they are featured in, they can also be used for any other chapter in the book. In addition to the specific vocabulary activities offered in this guide, following are some general vocabulary strategies to consider when teaching new vocabulary to students.

▶ Create Word Logs.

Students should be encouraged to keep Word Logs that they can use to record the vocabulary they identify for the Personalizing Vocabulary activity of the two-page lesson plan in this guide. The Word Log can be a spiral notebook divided by letters of the alphabet with a second section for phrases. Students can write definitions, sentences, or draw or cut out from magazines pictures to aid them in understanding and remembering.

▶ Pronounce Vocabulary Words and Phrases.

It is critical to pronounce vocabulary words and phrases for ESL/ELL students. As in the case of reading to your students, pronouncing new words and phrases allows students to grow accustomed to cadence and rhythm. When reviewing the pronunciation of the vocabulary words and phrases, you may wish to:

- pronounce each word and phrase for your students and have them listen to the pronunciation.
- pronounce each word and phrase for your students and ask your students to repeat each one.
- pronounce each word and phrase for your students and then have your students repeat them all in a choral read.
- provide a phonetic spelling for students to use in addition to the strategies mentioned above.

▶ Think About the Topic.

Help students make a connection between the new vocabulary word or phrase and a word or phrase in their own language. This allows them to see the word or phrase in their native language and aids in retention. Suggest also that ESL/ELL students refer to their first language for cognates or similar words.

▶ Monitor Comprehension.

Students have several opportunities to learn the academic vocabulary that appears in the Student Edition. However, students are not always comfortable or familiar with all of the words and phrases used in daily conversation, such as idiomatic expressions and colloquialisms. Always ask students if they understand the words and phrases that you use during the course of your lesson delivery. Your inquiry can be after a few sentences or after the use of a word or expression that you are unsure your students understand, but it should be frequent.

ESL/ELL

Chapter 1 — What Is History? pages 2–13

Introducing the Chapter

Tapping Prior Knowledge
Ask students to preview the chapter by reading the headings and subheadings and by looking at the art and photos (on pages 2, 4, and 7 of the Student Edition), the map (on page 9 of the Student Edition), and the timeline (on page 11 of the Student Edition). Then, direct students to the chapter title What Is History? on page 3 of the Student Edition. Ask students, *What is history? Why are historical events important to the world today?*

Preteaching Vocabulary
Personalizing Vocabulary Begin by asking students to preview the chapter for five unfamiliar words or phrases and to record them in their Word Logs. Once students have identified these words and phrases, ask them to use their dictionaries to define them.

Identifying Essential Vocabulary Go over the pronunciation and meaning of each word and phrase in the box below. Then, ask students to work with a partner to write the sentence where they find the word or phrase in the chapter and then replace the word or phrase with a word they are familiar with. Students may wish to consult their language dictionaries as they rewrite the sentences.

Word or Phrase	Meaning
set out	to start on a trip (p.4)
swept across	to move quickly and with force (p.4)
quest	long search for something (p.5)
forced	to make people do something they do not want to do (p.5)
age	a time in history (p.5)

Applying Content Knowledge

From the Chapter: Learn More About It (page 8)
Ask students to read Learn More About It: The Trojan War on page 8 of the Student Edition. Then, distribute the Who, What, Why, Where, When, and How chart on page 72 of this guide. Ask students to work with a partner to complete the chart using the information from Learn More About It.

Organizing Information
Distribute copies of the Spider Web on page 73 of this guide. Use the chapter title, **What Is History?** as the central topic. Ask students to label the spokes of their webs. **History Is All About Change, How Historians Learn About the Past**, and **Maps Show the Way**. Then, ask students to list key details that they learned about each heading.

Using Visuals
Ask students to read Maps Show the Way on page 9 of the Student Edition and to study the world map. Then, distribute a world map. Ask students to label the continents and the oceans and then to mark their continent in a special way.

Note-taking
Ask students to work with a partner to think of a historical event that they believe was among the most exciting things that ever happened in the world. Have students research the historical event on the Internet and share their research with the class. Ask students, *Why did you choose the event that you chose?*

2   Unit 1 • World History

Assessing Content Knowledge

Ask students to respond to the following questions. You may wish to encourage students with higher language proficiency to help beginning level students understand the questions.

Beginning Level Questions

Encourage students at this level to think about the answers to these questions and offer short verbal responses.

1. Look at page 4. What is another word for *change*? (revolution)
2. Look at the Remember margin note on page 5. What are the three basic human needs? (food, clothing, and shelter)
3. Look at the four photos on page 7. What do the photos show? (artifacts used by ancient civilizations as weapons and for preparing food)
4. Look at the map on page 9. How many continents are there? (seven)
5. Look at the timeline on page 11. When was the Industrial Revolution? (A.D. 1700–1850)

Intermediate Level Questions

Encourage students at this level to offer verbal responses or short written responses to the following questions.

1. Look at the section entitled History Is All About Change. About 500 years ago, what was a big change in the way that people pictured the world? (People came to understand that the true shape of our planet is round, not flat.)
2. Look at the section entitled History Is All About Change. What kinds of danger did the Sumerians have to face? (the dangers of nature, like floods)
3. Look at the section entitled How Historians Learn About the Past. What is the purpose of artifacts? (to help historians learn about the past)
4. Look at the section entitled Maps Show the Way. What do maps show? (Maps show how countries have changed; how groups of people have moved; that cities were built along rivers and on seacoasts; and how waterways made it possible for different people to come together.)
5. Look at the timeline on page 11. What is the oldest civilization? (Sumerians)

Advanced Level Questions

Encourage students at this level to provide written responses in complete sentences to the following questions.

1. What does history tell about the world? (History tells how people of different times and places lived. It also tells about the discoveries that were made; the cities and nations that were built; and the art and music that was created.)
2. Why did many countries try to fight imperialism? (People wanted to control their own lands and lives.)
3. Why is it important to study the past? (Answers will vary. Possible answers might include that knowing what happened can help keep history from repeating itself.)
4. What are three reasons to make maps? (Maps help you understand the world, to find your way, and to show landforms, weather, continents, countries, and cities.)
5. Why do you think some civilizations last longer than others? (Answers will vary. Students' answers might include good leaders, resources, protection, armies, and inventions.)

Closing the Chapter

Ask students to use the Spider Web they completed for the Organizing Information activity on page 2 of this guide to write a summary about what they learned.

ESL/ELL

Early Humans: The Story Begins
pages 14–25

▶ Introducing the Chapter

Tapping Prior Knowledge
Ask students to preview the chapter by reading the headings and subheadings and by looking at the art and photos (on pages 14, 18, 19, and 21 of the Student Edition), the timeline (on page 22 of the Student Edition), and the maps (on page 23 of the Student Edition). Direct students to the chapter title, Early Humans: The Story Begins on page 15 of the Student Edition. Encourage students to think about what they might have previously learned, read, or seen about Stone Age people. Ask students, *How do you think the early humans lived?*

Preteaching Vocabulary
Personalizing Vocabulary Begin by asking students to preview the chapter for five unfamiliar words or phrases and to record them in their Word Logs. Once students have identified these words and phrases, ask them to use their dictionaries to define them.

Identifying Essential Vocabulary Go over the pronunciation and meaning of each word and phrase in the box below. Then, ask each student to write a sentence for each word and phrase. Ask students to rewrite their sentences, leaving a blank space in place of the vocabulary word or phrase. Then, have students exchange sentences with a partner and fill in the blanks in the sentences their partner wrote.

Word or Phrase	Meaning
spread out	to cover a large area (p.15)
scattered about	spread over a wide area (p.15)
settle down	to start living in a place and plan to stay there (p.16)
for good	permanently; will always be this way (p.16)
counted on	depend on (p.16)
ready food supply	food that can be used quickly (p.17)
tame	train (p.17)

▶ Applying Content Knowledge

From the Chapter: Learn More About It (page 16)
Ask students to read Learn More About It: Cave Artwork on page 16 of the Student Edition. Then, have students look at the cave painting on page 14 of the Student Edition. Ask students, *What was special about cave artwork?* Remind them that cave artwork tells stories that give interesting information about the people who created them and the times they lived in. Ask students, *Why do you think people painted on cave walls?*

Using Manipulatives
Ask students to study the timeline on page 22 of the Student Edition. Have students work in small groups and write three questions from the information on the timeline. Then, distribute index cards and have students write each question on the front of an index card and the answer to that question on the back of the index card. Students can use the cards to practice answering questions about the agricultural revolution.

Using Visuals
Ask students to review The Middle East: Then and The Middle East: Now maps on page 23 of the Student Edition. Then, distribute the Venn diagram on page 74 of this guide. Ask students to label the sections **The Middle East: Then, Both,** and **The Middle East: Now.** Then, have students compare and contrast the Middle East then and the Middle East now by listing details in the appropriate sections of the diagram. Ask students to use their completed Venn diagrams to write a summary. Students may wish to use this model as a topic sentence: *The Middle East then was different from the Middle East now because…*

Personalizing the Lesson
Distribute the Timeline on page 75 of this guide. To develop more familiarity with timelines, ask students to create a personal timeline by recording five to ten important events in their lives. Then, have students illustrate their timelines with drawings, photos, or magazine cutouts.

4   Unit 1 • World History

ESL/ELL

▶ Assessing Content Knowledge

Ask students to respond to the following questions. You may wish to encourage students with higher language proficiency to help beginning level students understand the questions.

Beginning Level Questions

Encourage students at this level to think about the answers to these questions and offer short verbal responses.

1. Look at the picture on page 14. Where is this painting? (on a cave wall in Lascaux, France)
2. Look at page 17. What kinds of animals did people learn to tame? (dogs, cows, goats, sheep, and pigs)
3. Look at page 20. What eight lands were located along the great rivers of the Middle East? (Jordan, Syria, Iraq, Iran, Kuwait, Lebanon, Israel, and Turkey)
4. Look at the timeline on page 22. What happened in 4000 B.C.? (Rice farming developed in China.)
5. Look at the maps of the Middle East on page 23. What are the names of the bodies of water? (the Nile River, the Tigris River, and the Euphrates River; the Persian Gulf; the Black Sea, the Caspian Sea, the Arabian Sea, the Red Sea, and the Mediterranean Sea)

Intermediate Level Questions

Encourage students at this level to offer verbal responses or short written responses to the following questions.

1. Look at the section entitled The Hunters. Why was this first period called the Ice Age? (Most of the world was frozen and covered with glaciers.)
2. Look at the section entitled The Hunters. Why were the people and their way of life called the Stone Age? (because the people of the time used stone in their tools and weapons)
3. Look at the section entitled The Farmers. Why did the Ice Age end? (The glaciers began melting.)
4. Look at the section entitled The Agricultural Revolution. What were some of the crafts that people learned? (weaving, pottery, and spinning)
5. Look at the section entitled The Fertile Crescent. What was the Fertile Crescent? (land where the earliest known farming occurred along the great rivers of the Middle East)

Advanced Level Questions

Encourage students at this level to provide written responses in complete sentences to the following questions.

1. What happened as glaciers moved? (As glaciers moved, they pushed soil and rocks out of their way and many valley and lakes were formed.)
2. Why was life such a struggle for people in the Ice Age? (They could never settle down for good. Without a good hunt, they would die.)
3. Why was the agricultural revolution important? (It created occupations like farming, building, weaving, pottery, spinning, and trading.)
4. What was Mesopotamia? (Mesopotamia was the land between the Tigris and Euphrates Rivers.)
5. Why do archaeologists think Jericho was attacked and captured around 7000 B.C.? (The style of architecture changed from rounded mud and brick houses to houses with square corners, suggesting that a new group of people must have taken over and settled there.)

▶ Closing the Chapter

Distribute the Outline on page 76 of this guide. Write the following headings on the chalkboard and ask students to copy them onto their outlines. Have students complete the outline by filling in the important details discussed under each heading. Then, ask students to write a paragraph that summarizes what they learned.

> **Topic: Early Humans**
>   I. The Hunters
>   A.
>   B.
>   C.
>   II. The Farmers
>   A.
>   B.
>   C.
>   III. The Agricultural Revolution
>   A.
>   B.
>   C.
>   IV. The Fertile Crescent
>   A.
>   B.
>   C.

Chapter 3: Sumerians: The First Great Civilization
pages 28–39

Introducing the Chapter

Tapping Prior Knowledge
Ask students to preview the chapter by reading the headings and subheadings and by looking at the art and photos (on pages 28, 32, 33, and 36 of the Student Edition), the map (on page 30 of the Student Edition), the chart (on page 34 of the Student Edition), and the timeline (on page 37 of the Student Edition). Then, direct students to the art on pages 28, 33, and 36 of the Student Edition. Ask students, *What do you know about the civilization of the Sumerians from these pictures?* Encourage students to discuss their observations and conclusions. Ask students, *What might the Sumerian people have been like? How might they have lived?*

Preteaching Vocabulary
Personalizing Vocabulary Begin by asking students to preview the chapter for five unfamiliar words or phrases and to record them in their Word Logs. Once students have identified these words and phrases, ask them to use their dictionaries to define them.

Identifying Essential Vocabulary Go over the pronunciation and meaning of each word and phrase in the box below. Then, provide sheets of graph paper with large boxes and ask students to use the words and phrases to create a crossword puzzle. Have students use sentences from the text as the definitions. Then, ask each student to exchange his or her puzzle with a partner to be completed.

Word or Phrase	Meaning
washed up	to come onto the beach or shore (p.29)
rich bottom-soil	land that is good for growing plants (p.29)
washed away	destroyed by water or flood (p.30)
river banks	the land on the side of the river (p.30)
goods	things made to be sold (p.31)
keep track of	to pay attention to something so you know what is happening to it (p.33)
nobles	people in the highest social group in some countries (p.36)

Applying Content Knowledge

From the Chapter: Words From the Past (page 34)
Ask students to read Words From the Past: How Writing Changed on page 34 of the Student Edition. Distribute the Sequence of Events chart on page 77 of this guide. Ask students to work in groups to sequence the steps of how writing changed. You may wish to have students make their own pictographs and cuneiforms. You might wish to suggest simple concepts like *tree, house, cat,* and *flower* and then encourage students to think of others. Ask students, *Why do you think the way people wrote changed?*

Using Visuals
Ask students to study the timeline entitled Sumer, 5000 B.C. to 2000 B.C. on page 37 of the Student Edition. Then, ask students to use the key dates and information from the timeline to write a paragraph about the Sumerians.

Organizing Information
Distribute the Outline on page 76 of this guide. Write the following headings on the chalkboard and ask students to copy them onto their outlines. Have students complete the outline by filling in the important details discussed under each heading.

> Topic: The Sumerians
> I. Gifts From the Sumerians
>   A.
>   B.
> II. Life in Sumer
>   A.
>   B.
> III. Attack on Ur
>   A.
>   B.

Personalizing the Lesson
Ask students to read Other Gifts From the Sumerians on page 35 of the Student Edition. Then, ask students to decide which Sumerian invention—the wheel or writing—is important for us today. Have students give three reasons to support their choices.

Assessing Content Knowledge

Ask students to respond to the following questions. You may wish to encourage students with higher language proficiency to help beginning level students understand the questions.

Beginning Level Questions

Encourage students at this level to think about the answers to these questions and offer short verbal responses.

1. Look at the map on page 30. What river is Ur near? (the Euphrates River)
2. Look at page 32. What was the name of one of Sumer's greatest city-states? (Ur)
3. Look at page 33. What was the greatest gift that the Sumerians gave to the world? (the invention of writing)
4. Look at the chart on page 34. What information does the third column tell? (what late pictographs looked like)
5. Look at the timeline on page 37. When was Sumer conquered by the Babylonians? (2000 B.C.)

Intermediate Level Questions

Encourage students at this level to offer verbal responses or short written responses to the following questions.

1. Look at the section entitled Trading. What kinds of treasures did the trading boats bring from other lands? (gold, silver, pearls, and copper)
2. Look at the section entitled Villages Grow Into City-States. Why was the ziggurat built? (to honor the god who watched over the city)
3. Look at the section entitled The Invention of Writing. Why do we know a great deal about the Sumerians? (Sumerian scribes wrote down their ideas and kept records.)
4. Look at the section entitled Life in Sumer. Who were the highest classes in the Sumerian culture? (king, priests, scribes, and nobles)
5. Look at the section entitled Attack on Ur. Why did Sumer grow weak? (The Sumerian city-states fought with each other.)

Advanced Level Questions

Encourage students at this level to provide written responses in complete sentences to the following questions.

1. Why was flooding of the rivers both good and bad? (It was good because it put rich soil on the land and made it good for farming. It was bad because it could wash away whole villages, causing many people to die.)
2. How can a city also be a state? (It has its own government and surrounding land, makes its own laws, and has its own army.)
3. Why was each Sumerian village built around a temple? (The people believed a god or goddess lived in the temple and protected the village.)
4. Why did the Sumerians invent writing? (They needed a way to keep track of what they owned.)
5. Why were the Sumerians' ideas and inventions important for future civilizations? (All civilizations that followed used inventions of the Sumerians.)

Closing the Chapter

Ask students, *Why was Sumer a great civilization?* Ask students to use the Outline they completed for the Organizing Information activity on page 6 of this guide to write a summary about why Sumer was a great civilization.

Ancient Egypt: Land of the Pharaohs
pages 40–51

▶ Introducing the Chapter

Tapping Prior Knowledge
Ask students to preview the chapter by reading the headings and subheadings and by looking at the art and photos (on pages 40, 46, and 49 of the Student Edition), the map (on page 43 of the Student Edition), and the timeline (on page 48 of the Student Edition). Then, ask students to rewrite each of the Learning Objectives on page 40 of the Student Edition in the form of a question. For example, the first one could be rewritten as Why did people settle along the Nile River? Then, ask students which of these questions they can already answer. Tell students that the questions that they are currently unable to answer they will learn the answers to as they read the chapter. Ask students, *What would you like to know about ancient Egypt?*

Preteaching Vocabulary
Personalizing Vocabulary Begin by asking students to preview the chapter for five unfamiliar words or phrases and to record them in their Word Logs. Once students have identified these words and phrases, ask them to use their dictionaries to define them.

Identifying Essential Vocabulary Go over the pronunciation and meaning of each word in the box below. Then, ask students to combine one of these words with a vocabulary word from the list of Words to Know on page 41 of the Student Edition to create a sentence. Write the following sentence on the chalkboard for students to model: <u>Pharaohs</u> lived <u>splendid</u> lives.

▶ Applying Content Knowledge

From the Chapter: Words From the Past (page 49)
Ask students to read Words From the Past: The Rosetta Stone on page 49 of the Student Edition. Distribute the Who, What, Why, Where, When, and How chart on page 72 of this guide. Ask students to work with a partner to complete the chart for Words From the Past: The Rosetta Stone. Students may wish to write **Who Was Involved** underneath the word **Who** in the chart, **What Happened** underneath the word **What** in the chart, **Where It Happened** underneath the word **Where** in the chart, **When It Happened** underneath the word **When** in the chart, **Why It Happened** underneath the word **Why** in the chart, and **How It Happened** underneath the word **How** in the chart.

Note-taking
Distribute the Outline on page 76 of this guide. Ask students to outline the chapter using the headings and subheadings from the chapter. Have students complete the outline by filling in the important details discussed under each heading.

Organizing Information
Distribute the Spider Web on page 73 of this guide. For the central topic, have students write **The Egyptians**. Ask students to label the spokes of their webs **Egyptian Mummies**, **Egyptian Life**, **Egyptian Religion**, and **Egyptian Inventions**. Then, ask students to list key details from the chapter in the appropriate sections of their webs.

Word or Phrase	Meaning
wonders	things that make you feel admiration and surprise (p.40)
plain	a large area of flat, dry land (p.41)
splendid	beautiful and impressive (p.44)
chisel	a tool used to cut wood or stone (p.45)
record	information that is written down so that it can be looked at in the future (p.45)

ESL/ELL

▶ Assessing Content Knowledge

Ask students to respond to the following questions. You may wish to encourage students with higher language proficiency to help beginning level students understand the questions.

Beginning Level Questions

Encourage students at this level to think about the answers to these questions and offer short verbal responses.

1. Look at page 41. What is the name of the great river in Egypt? (the Nile River)
2. Look at the map on page 43. What are the two cities on the Nile River? (Memphis and Thebes)
3. Look at page 43. Who was the first pharaoh? (King Menes)
4. Look at page 44. What was the most famous pyramid? (the Great Pyramid near Cairo)
5. Look at page 47. What did Egyptians use to make paper? (a reed called papyrus)

Intermediate Level Questions

Encourage students at this level to offer verbal responses or short written responses to the following questions.

1. Look at the section entitled Along the Nile. How did farmers learn to use the floods to help them? (They learned to save up some of the flood waters, so they could water their crops during the rest of the year.)
2. Look at the section entitled The Pyramids. What was the purpose of the pyramids? (to serve as tombs for the pharaohs)
3. Look at the section entitled Egyptian Life and Religion. How do we know that Egyptians were concerned about the way they looked? (Drawings and statues show women with long, dark hair worn in many braids and ringlets, as well as people wearing makeup.)
4. Look at the section entitled Egyptian Inventions. What did the Egyptians use to make paper? (papyrus)
5. Look at the section entitled Words From the Past. How did the Rosetta Stone help archaeologists and historians? (It helped them to translate papyrus rolls and understand ancient Egyptian hieroglyphics.)

Advanced Level Questions

Encourage students at this level to provide written responses in complete sentences to the following questions.

1. Why was the Nile River Valley important to Egyptians? (It provided fertile soil and water.)
2. How have the pyramids helped archaeologists? (The pictures on the walls of the tombs and the artifacts inside give information about the Egyptians who lived there.)
3. Why are pyramids considered one of the wonders of the world? (Answers will vary. Possible answers might include ideas about the size, the Egyptians' ability to build such a structure, and the fact that they are still standing today.)
4. What are four things we know about the Egyptians' lives? (Answers will vary. Possible answers might include burial information, belief in many gods, concern for appearance, belief in an afterlife, their belief in their gods, their system of writing, and their inventions.)
5. How did the Rosetta Stone become the key to understanding hieroglyphics? (The Rosetta Stone had one message written in three languages. If you can understand one of the languages, you can use the information as a key to translating the others.)

▶ Closing the Chapter

Ask students to answer the questions they wrote for the Tapping Prior Knowledge activity on page 8 of this guide. Have students use the answers to their questions to write a summary about what they learned.

ESL/ELL

Mediterranean Kingdoms

pages 52–67

Introducing the Chapter

Tapping Prior Knowledge
Ask students to preview the chapter by reading the headings and subheadings and by looking at the art and photos (on pages 52, 55, 57, 60, and 64 of the Student Edition), the map (on page 55 of the Student Edition), and the timelines (on pages 56, 59, 62, and 65 of the Student Edition). Then, direct students to the timelines on pages 56, 59, 62, and 65 of the Student Edition. What information can students learn from studying timelines before they read? Encourage students to use the information from the timelines to suggest what the chapter might be about. Ask students, *What do these four timelines tell about the different groups who fought for control of this land?*

Preteaching Vocabulary
Personalizing Vocabulary Begin by asking students to preview the chapter for five unfamiliar words or phrases and to record them in their Word Logs. Once students have identified these words and phrases, ask them to use their dictionaries to define them.

Identifying Essential Vocabulary Go over the pronunciation and meaning of each word and phrase in the box below. Then, distribute an index card to each student. Ask each student to write a question on the index card using one or more of the vocabulary words. Then, have students select a partner to exchange cards with and have each student answer his or her partner's question.

Word or Phrase	Meaning
stand for	to have a position or opinion (p.56)
tribes	groups of people who are the same race and culture and who live together under a leader (p.58)
split	divide into two or more groups (p.58)
fierce	angry and frightening (p.65)

Applying Content Knowledge

From the Chapter: Words From the Past (page 57)
Ask students to read Words From the Past: The Ten Commandments on page 57 of the Student Edition. Then, distribute the Spider Web on page 73 of this guide. For the central topic, have students write **The Ten Commandments.** Then, ask students to write a heading for each paragraph on the spokes of the webs. Have students complete their webs using key details from the selection.

Using Visuals
Distribute the Timeline on page 75 of this guide. As students read about each kingdom, have them record each of the kingdoms on the timeline, along with the dates when those kingdoms occupied the land. You might wish to ask students to create a symbol, or icon, for each of the different groups to add to their timelines.

Organizing Information
Distribute the Description Web on page 78 of this guide. Ask students to work in groups to complete a Description Web for each of the civilizations discussed in the chapter. Ask students to write the name of the civilization they are working on in the central circle. Then, ask students to write the following headings in the surrounding circles: **Group, Time, Location, Ruler, Cities, Religion, Occupations,** and **Accomplishments.** Ask students to complete their webs by writing key details under each heading. When students have completed this activity, they should each have five Description Webs—one each for the Phoenicians, the Israelites, the Babylonians, the Hittites, and the Assyrians.

Using Manipulatives
Distribute index cards to students. Have students write the name of a civilization on the front of an index card and one or two interesting facts about that civilization on the back of the index card. Then, have students work in pairs to practice identifying the civilization referred to by the facts on each card.

Assessing Content Knowledge

Ask students to respond to the following questions. You may wish to encourage students with higher language proficiency to help beginning level students understand the questions.

Beginning Level Questions

Encourage students at this level to think about the answers to these questions and offer short verbal responses.

1. Look at page 53. What did the Phoenicians invent? (the alphabet)
2. Look at the map on page 55. What were the cities of Phoenicia? (Byblos, Sidon, and Tyre)
3. Look at page 56. Who was the father of the Israelites? (Abraham)
4. Look at the timeline on page 59. What happened to Israel in 722 B.C.? (Israel was conquered by the Assyrians.)
5. Look at page 61. Who created the Code of Hammurabi? (Hammurabi, one of the greatest kings of Babylonia)

Intermediate Level Questions

Encourage students at this level to offer verbal responses or short written responses to the following questions.

1. Look at the section entitled Phoenician Inventions. What are two things that the Phoenicians invented? (the Phoenician alphabet and dye to color cloth)
2. Look at the section entitled The Ancient Israelites: Under One God. What happened to the Israelites in Egypt? (They were treated as slaves until Moses led them out of Egypt into the desert.)
3. Look at the section entitled The Babylonians: The Rule of Law. What was Babylon? (It was one of the greatest cities of the ancient world, and the capital city of the Babylonians.)
4. Look at the section entitled The Hittites. Who were the Hittites? (warriors who came to the eastern Mediterranean around 2000 B.C.)
5. Look at the section entitled The Assyrians. What were the Assyrians known for? (Answers will vary. Possible answers might include their great army, their cruelty, their siege machines, and their library, buildings, and statues.)

Advanced Level Questions

Encourage students at this level to provide written responses in complete sentences to the following questions.

1. Why did the Phoenicians set up colonies? (Phoenicians lived in the colonies and colonies traded with the Phoenicians and paid taxes to the Phoenician homeland.)
2. What characterized the religious beliefs of most people in the Mediterranean? (They worshiped many gods.)
3. Why is the Code of Hammurabi important today? (Some of the ideas about laws and justice are included in our own laws today, and they were created to protect the rights of individual citizens.)
4. Why do you think the Hittite civilization signed a treaty with Egypt? (Answers will vary. Possible answers include mutual respect, being tired from years of fighting, and the desire for peace.)
5. Why do you think different groups wanted to conquer other groups? (Answers will vary. Possible answers include issues of power, control, wealth, or possession of land.)

Closing the Chapter

Ask students to use the Description Webs they created for the Organizing Information activity on page 10 of this guide to write a summary about what they learned.

ESL/ELL

Early Civilizations of India, China, and the Americas

pages 68–83

Introducing the Chapter

Tapping Prior Knowledge
Ask students to preview the chapter by reading the headings and subheadings and by looking at the art and photos (on pages 68, 72, and 80 of the Student Edition), the maps (on pages 70, 75, and 79 of the Student Edition), and the timelines (on pages 74 and 81 of the Student Edition). Then, direct students to the maps on pages 70, 75, and 79 of the Student Edition. Distribute the KWL chart on page 79 of this guide and ask students to use the maps to complete the **K** and the **W** columns of the chart. Ask students, *What do you want to know about India from studying the maps? China? the Americas?*

Preteaching Vocabulary
Personalizing Vocabulary Begin by asking students to preview the chapter for five unfamiliar words or phrases and to record them in their Word Logs. Once students have identified these words and phrases, ask them to use their dictionaries to define them.

Identifying Essential Vocabulary Go over the pronunciation and meaning of each word and phrase in the box below. Then, distribute the four-column chart on page 80 of this guide. Have students create a chart using the following headings: **Word or Phrase, Meaning Clues From the Text, Definition,** and **My Sentence.**

Word or Phrase	Meaning
stood	stayed (p.70)
conquer	to control a land or country by attacking people and fighting a war (p.71)
flee	to leave quickly to escape danger (p.72)
sacred	thought to be holy (p.73)
weakened	to become less powerful (p.73)
cut off from	difficult to get to (p.74)
made it possible	cause something to happen (p.75)

Applying Content Knowledge

From the Chapter: Great Names in History (page 77)
Ask students to read Great Names in History: Confucius on page 77 of the Student Edition. Suggest that students work in groups to research five of the teachings of Confucius. Then, ask students to share their research with the class.

Note-taking
Distribute the Timeline on page 75 of this guide. Ask students to read the section entitled Chinese Dynasties and organize the dynasties on their timelines. Have students write two or three details about each dynasty next to the name of the dynasty on their timelines.

Organizing Information
Distribute the Outline on page 76 of this guide. As students read about the early civilization of India, ask them to use the headings and subheadings from the chapter to complete their outlines.

Summarizing
Distribute the Venn Diagram on page 74 of this guide. Ask students to label the sections **The North Americans, Both,** and **The South Americans.** Then, have students compare and contrast the North Americans and the South Americans by listing details in the appropriate sections of the diagram. Ask students to use their completed Venn diagrams to write a summary. Students may wish to use this model as a topic sentence: *The North Americans were different from the South Americans because…*

Assessing Content Knowledge

Ask students to respond to the following questions. You may wish to encourage students with higher language proficiency to help beginning level students understand the questions.

Beginning Level Questions

Encourage students at this level to think about the answers to these questions and offer short verbal responses.

1. Look at the map on page 70. What river runs through Mohenjo-Daro? (the Indus River)
2. Look at the timeline on page 74. What happened to ancient India in 321 B.C.? (the Maurya Empire began)
3. Look at the map on page 75. What two rivers run through the Shang Dynasty of China? (the Chang Jiang [Yangtze] and the Huang He [Yellow] Rivers)
4. Look at the photo on page 80. Who built the temple? (the Maya)
5. Look at pages 80–81. Where were the Olmec and Maya civilizations? (Mexico and Central America)

Intermediate Level Questions

Encourage students at this level to offer verbal responses or short written responses to the following questions.

1. Look at the section entitled India's Caste System. What did the Aryans do to all people? (They divided them into four social classes, or castes.)
2. Look at the section entitled The Buddhist Religion. What does the Buddhist religion teach? (It teaches that the sacred life is found in unselfishness.)
3. Look at the section entitled China: The Huang He Valley. What were two important beliefs of the Chinese? (Answers will vary. Possible answers include honor toward home, family, and land; courtesy; and a special feeling for their ancestors.)
4. Look at the section entitled Chinese Dynasties. What were four of the great dynasties in China? (Shang, Zhou, Qin, and Han)
5. Look at the section entitled The Americas. How do many scientists believe the Native Americans came to the Americas? (by traveling across a bridge of land and ice at the Bering Strait that would have stretched 56 miles between Asia and Alaska)

Advanced Level Questions

Encourage students at this level to provide written responses in complete sentences to the following questions.

1. How was Mohenjo-Daro similar to cities today? (Mohenjo-Daro is similar to cities today because it had straight main streets, covered drainage systems under the streets, brick houses, apartments, swimming pools, and bath houses.)
2. Why was Asoka, the Mauryan emperor, a good ruler? (He followed Buddha's teachings about brotherly love, taught that all people and animals were to be loved, and treated all people more equally than the Hindu caste system did.)
3. Why didn't the Chinese culture change for many thousands of years? (People honored the ways of their ancestors, and the land was cut off from the rest of the world.)
4. What are the two different beliefs about the origins of the North Americans? (One belief says that they have always lived in the Americas. Another belief says that they traveled from Asia over a land bridge of ice.)
5. What was impressive about the way the Olmecs did their carvings? (The Olmecs made their carvings without metal tools and without the wheel.)

Closing the Chapter

Ask students to complete the L column of the KWL charts that they began for the Tapping Prior Knowledge activity on page 12 of this guide. Then, have students use their completed KWL charts to write a summary about what they learned.

ESL/ELL

Greek City-States and the Golden Age
pages 86–99

▶ Introducing the Chapter

Tapping Prior Knowledge
Ask students to preview the chapter by reading the headings and subheadings and by looking at the art and photos (on pages 86, 91, 96, and 97 of the Student Edition), the map (on page 88 of the Student Edition), and the timeline (on page 97 of the Student Edition). Ask students what the phrase *the Golden Age* means. Encourage students to use their bilingual dictionaries to define any words in the expression that may be unfamiliar. Have students suggest possible meanings of the phrase and work with students to arrive at a clear explanation of the phrase. Then, ask students, *What might the Golden Age have been like?*

Preteaching Vocabulary
Personalizing Vocabulary Begin by asking students to preview the chapter for five unfamiliar words or phrases and to record them in their Word Logs. Once students have identified these words and phrases, ask them to use their dictionaries to define them.

Identifying Essential Vocabulary Go over the pronunciation and meaning of each word and phrase in the box below. Then, ask students to create a sentence by combining one of the words or phrases from the box below with one of the words from the list of Words to Know on page 87 of the Student Edition. You may wish to model this for students using the following example: <u>Citizens</u> had <u>a say in</u> the government in Athens.

Word or Phrase	Meaning
little use for	no respect for (p.90)
a say in	the right to participate in making decisions (p.93)
flowered	to reach a high level of achievement (p.95)
works	books, plays, paintings, sculptures, or music (p.96)

▶ Applying Content Knowledge

From the Chapter: Learn More About It (page 92)
Ask students to read Learn More About It: Greek Religion on page 92 of the Student Edition. Then, distribute the Who, What, Why, Where, When, and How chart on page 72 of this guide. Have each student select one Greek god or goddess to research. Then, ask each student to complete the Who, What, Why, Where, When, and How chart with information he or she found about the god or goddess he or she chose, use the chart to write a one-paragraph summary of the information on the chart, and report the findings to the class. As students listen to each presentation, ask them to take notes on the attributes of each god and goddess. Ask students, *How are the gods and goddesses alike? How are they different?*

Note-taking
Distribute the Outline on page 76 of this guide. As students read the chapter, ask them to use the headings and subheadings from the chapter to complete their outlines.

Using Visuals
Distribute the Venn diagram on page 74 of this guide. Ask students to label the sections **Sparta**, **Athens**, and **Both**. Then, have students compare and contrast Sparta and Athens by listing details in the appropriate sections of the diagram. Ask students to use their completed Venn diagrams to write a summary. Students may wish to use this as a model topic sentences: *Sparta and Athens were different from each other because…*

Organizing Information
Ask students to review The Persian Wars on page 94 of the Student Edition. Then, distribute the Sequence of Events chart on page 77 of this guide. Ask students to take notes about the Persian Wars and then sequence the events of the Persian Wars on their charts.

Assessing Content Knowledge

Ask students to respond to the following questions. You may wish to encourage students with higher language proficiency to help beginning level students understand the questions.

Beginning Level Questions

Encourage students at this level to think about the answers to these questions and offer short verbal responses.

1. Look at the map on page 88. What countries and cities are shown? (Countries: Macedonia, Lydia, Ancient Greece, Egypt; Cities: Olympia, Sparta, Athens, Marathon)
2. Look at page 90. What was the Acropolis? (a high hill where the Greeks built temples and theaters)
3. Look at page 95. What was another name for the Golden Age? (the Age of Pericles)
4. Look at page 96. What are some English words taken from the Greek language? (astronomy, biology, geography, geology, music, theater, drama, comedy, tragedy, athlete)
5. Look at the timeline on page 97. When did the Persian Wars take place? (546–479 B.C.)

Intermediate Level Questions

Encourage students at this level to offer verbal responses or short written responses to the following questions.

1. Look at the section entitled Greek City-States. In what countries did the Greeks build cities? (Greece, Italy, France, Spain, Portugal, Turkey)
2. Look at the section entitled Athens and Sparta. What happened to a Spartan boy when he turned seven? (He was handed over to the government to be raised as a soldier.)
3. Look at the section entitled The Golden Age. Why was the Golden Age important? (Athens flowered by continuing its democratic government and rebuilding the Parthenon.)
4. Look at the section entitled The Peloponnesian War. How did Sparta win the war against Athens? (A plague killed one fourth of the people in Athens, including Pericles.)
5. Look at the section entitled Gifts From the Greeks. What are three gifts from the Greeks? (Answers will vary. Possible answers might include Greek ideas in building; the works of Greek thinkers; their ideas about the sun, the Earth, and the stars; the concept of democracy; certain words in our language; and the Olympic games.)

Advanced Level Questions

Encourage students at this level to provide written responses in complete sentences to the following questions.

1. Why was trading an advantage for the Greeks? (They set up colonies and spread their culture to other lands.)
2. What was the main difference between Athens and Sparta? (Sparta was a military society, and Athens was an artistic, intellectual society that was more interested in enjoying life.)
3. Why did the people of Athens want to become citizens? (They wanted to have a say in the government.)
4. What led to the Peloponnesian War? (Sparta was angry that Athens had been collecting money from other Greek city-states, and both powers wanted to control Greece.)
5. What does "Future ages will wonder at us" mean? (Answers will vary. Answers should reflect awareness of the remarkable accomplishments of the Greeks.)

Closing the Chapter

Ask students to use the outline they completed for the Note-taking activity on page 14 of this guide to summarize what they learned.

ESL/ELL

Chapter 8: Alexander the Great

pages 100–109

▶ Introducing the Chapter

Tapping Prior Knowledge

Ask students to preview the chapter by reading the headings and subheadings and by looking at the art and photos (on pages 100 and 102 of the Student Edition), the map (on page 106 of the Student Edition), and the timeline (on page 107 of the Student Edition). Then, direct students to the map Alexander's Empire on page 106 of the Student Edition. Ask students to measure the distances and think about people crossing those countries on foot and on horses and conquering and controlling all of this land. Encourage students to discuss their own experience of traveling over long distances. Ask students, *What kinds of challenges might Alexander the Great have faced during his travels?*

Preteaching Vocabulary

Personalizing Vocabulary Begin by asking students to preview the chapter for five unfamiliar words or phrases and to record them in their Word Logs. Once students have identified these words and phrases, ask them to use their dictionaries to define them.

Identifying Essential Vocabulary Go over the pronunciation and meaning of each word and phrase in the box below. Then, ask each student to write a sentence for each word and phrase. Then, ask students to rewrite their sentences, leaving a blank space in place of the vocabulary term. Have students trade sentences with a partner and fill in the blanks in the sentences their partner wrote.

Word or Phrase	Meaning
saw to it	did something (p.101)
two years saw	something happened during a two-year period of time (p.103)
swept	moved quickly and with force (p.103)
gotten even	harmed someone as much as he or she harmed you (p.105)
left his mark	became successful or famous (p.107)

▶ Applying Content Knowledge

From the Chapter: Learn More About It (page 104)

Ask students to read Learn More About It: Alexandria on page 104 of the Student Edition. Tell students to look at the second paragraph, which mentions the lighthouse, one of the wonders of the world. Ask students to work with a partner to research other wonders of the world. Ask students, *What are the other wonders of the world? What do you think makes them wonders of the world?* You may wish to ask students to illustrate the wonders of the world on a poster.

Note-taking

Ask students to read King Philip of Macedonia on pages 101–102 of the Student Edition. Then, discuss with students the difference between a fact and an opinion. Explain to students that a fact is a piece of information that can be measured or proven with evidence, and an opinion is an idea that other people can agree or disagree with. Then, have students copy five factual statements about Philip II and write an opinion for each of those facts. You might wish to provide the following example as a model: *Fact: Macedonia was ruled by a king named Philip II. Opinion: He was a brilliant king.*

Organizing Information

Distribute the Idea Web on page 81 of this guide. Ask students to write **Alexander the Great** as the central topic and words and phrases that describe Alexander the Great in the surrounding circles.

Note-taking

Distribute the Outline on page 76 of this guide. As students read the chapter, ask them to use the outline to fill in the headings and corresponding details about Alexander the Great.

ESL/ELL

▶ Assessing Content Knowledge

Ask students to respond to the following questions. You may wish to encourage students with higher language proficiency to help beginning level students understand the questions.

Beginning Level Questions

Encourage students at this level to think about the answers to these questions and offer short verbal responses.

1. Look at page 101. Who was the ruler of Macedonia? (King Phillip II)
2. Look at page 103. What did Alexander order his men to build? (a raised road over the sea to reach the city)
3. Look at page 105. Where was much of the Persian empire's wealth stored? (in the palaces of Persepolis)
4. Look at the map on page 106. What were the countries in Alexander's empire? (Macedonia, Greece, Egypt, Syria, and Persia)
5. Look at the timeline on page 107. What are two countries that Alexander the Great invaded or conquered? (Egypt and India)

Intermediate Level Questions

Encourage students at this level to offer verbal responses or short written responses to the following questions.

1. Look at the section entitled King Philip of Macedonia. How did King Philip change the economy of Macedonia? (He encouraged farming and trading and built roads.)
2. Look at the section entitled Philip's Son. What were some of the things Alexander was taught? (Answers will vary. Possible answers might include warfare, leadership, sports, cultures, and heroes.)
3. Look at the section entitled Alexander in Egypt. Why were the Egyptians happy that Alexander was the new ruler? (The Persians had been harsh rulers.)
4. Look at the section entitled Alexander in the Valley of Indus. Why didn't Alexander's men want to go deeper into India? (They were tired, and they wanted to go home.)
5. Look at the section entitled The Death of Alexander. How did Alexander envision Europe and Asia? (He imagined them as one big country united under his rule.)

Advanced Level Questions

Encourage students at this level to provide written responses in complete sentences to the following questions.

1. What influence did Philip have on the Macedonian army? (He built war machinery, and he taught men his new ways of fighting.)
2. What were some of Alexander's qualities? (Answers will vary. Possible answers might include his fearlessness, talent, ambition, love of power, and ability to command.)
3. What does Alexander's treatment of the people in Persepolis tell you about him? (Answers will vary. Possible answers might include ideas about his ruthlessness, power, leadership ability, cruelty, thoroughness, and vengefulness.)
4. Why was spreading Greek culture and ideas to the world a positive thing? (Answers will vary. Possible answers should reflect the extraordinary advancements the Greeks had made in knowledge and learning.)
5. Why did Alexander's empire break into smaller empires after he died? (There was no one man to hold it together, and he had set up rulers as he moved on to conquer more lands.)

▶ Closing the Chapter

Ask students to use the outline they completed for the Note-taking activity on page 16 of this guide to summarize what they learned.

ESL/ELL

The Rise of Rome
pages 110–131

▶ Introducing the Chapter

Tapping Prior Knowledge
Ask students to preview the chapter by reading the headings and subheadings and by looking at the art and photos (on pages 110, 114, 116, 123, 125, and 127 of the Student Edition), the maps (on pages 119 and 127 of the Student Edition), and the timelines (on pages 128 and 129 of the Student Edition). Then, direct students to the map on page 119 of the Student Edition. Ask students to name some of the present-day countries that are located in the area of the Roman Empire. Ask students, *How might the size and power of the Roman Empire have contributed to the rise of Rome?*

Preteaching Vocabulary
Personalizing Vocabulary Begin by asking students to preview the chapter for five unfamiliar words or phrases and to record them in their Word Logs. Once students have identified these words and phrases, ask them to use their dictionaries to define them.

Identifying Essential Vocabulary Go over the pronunciation and meaning of each word and phrase in the box below. Then, distribute the four-column chart on page 80 of this guide. Have students create a chart using the following headings: **Word or Phrase, Sentence From the Text, Synonym,** and **My Sentence.** You may wish to ask students to read Words From the Past: Borrowed Words on page 123 of the Student Edition, and add the words in italics to their charts.

Word or Phrase	Meaning
trade route	a way across land or water that is used for trading (p.113)
quarreled	to have angry arguments or disagreements (p.113)
sided with	to support a person or a group in an argument or fight (p.115)
plotted	to make a secret plan to harm a person or an organization (p.117)
flourish	to develop and be successful (p.118)
clashed	disagree (p.127)

▶ Applying Content Knowledge

From the Chapter: Great Names in History (page 114)
Ask students to read Great Names in History: Hannibal on page 114 of the Student Edition. Then, distribute the Idea Web on page 81 of this guide. Ask students to write **Hannibal** as the central topic and words and phrases that describe Hannibal and the things he did in the surrounding circles. Ask students, *Do you think that Hannibal was a good leader? Why or why not?*

Using Manipulatives
Distribute index cards to students. Have students write the name of a famous Roman leader on the front of an index card and one or two interesting facts about that leader on the back of the index card. Then, have students work in pairs to practice identifying the leaders referred to by the facts on each card.

Note-taking
Distribute the Outline on page 76 of this guide. Write the following headings on the chalkboard and ask students to copy them onto their outlines. As students read the chapter, ask them to use the outline to fill in the corresponding details.

> **Topic: The Rise of Rome**
> I. Early Rome
> II. The Roman Republic
>   A. Roman Warriors
>   B. The Provinces
> III. Julius Caesar
>   A.
>   B.
> IV. The Emperor Augustus
> V. Life in Rome

Organizing Information
Ask students to read Life in Rome on page 120 of the Student Edition. Then, have students work in small groups to create a travel brochure encouraging travelers to come to Rome. Ask students to think about the kinds of things that might attract tourists to Rome around 27 B.C. Ask students, *What places should tourists visit? What events should they see?*

Assessing Content Knowledge

Ask students to respond to the following questions. You may wish to encourage students with higher language proficiency to help beginning level students understand the questions.

Beginning Level Questions

Encourage students at this level to think about the answers to these questions and offer short verbal responses.

1. Look at page 112. For how many years was Rome ruled by Etruscan kings? (about 100 years)
2. Look at page 113. What was one of Rome's greatest enemies? (Carthage)
3. Look at page 116. Who was Julius Caesar? (the Roman general in the province of Gaul)
4. Look at the map on page 119. What sea did the Roman Empire circle completely? (the Mediterranean Sea)
5. Look at the timeline on page 129. What did the Romans do in 509 B.C.? (They set up the Republic.)

Intermediate Level Questions

Encourage students at this level to offer verbal responses or short written responses to the following questions.

1. Look at the section entitled Early Rome. What are three skills the Etruscans had? (They built a wall around the city; they drained nearby swamps, and they laid the first sewer.)
2. Look at the section entitled The Provinces. Why did Rome send large armies to each province? (to keep people in order)
3. Look at the section entitled Life in Rome. What are two things that the Romans built? (temples and public baths)
4. Look at the section entitled The End of the Empire. Why did the need for bigger armies start the fall of the Empire? (Bigger armies meant bigger taxes, and people were unable to pay them.)
5. Look at the timeline on page 129. What date marks the beginning of the Roman Empire? (27 B.C.)

Advanced Level Questions

Encourage students at this level to provide written responses in complete sentences to the following questions.

1. What is the main difference between the government of early Rome and the government of the Roman Empire? (Early Rome was ruled by Etruscan kings, and the Roman Republic was controlled by the people and the leaders they elected.)
2. Look at the maps on pages 119 and 127. What happened to the size of the Roman Empire? (It increased in size so much that it was divided into the Eastern Roman Empire and the Western Roman Empire.)
3. Why was the period after the civil wars called the Pax Romana? (It was a time of Roman peace during which the Roman Empire flourished as never before.)
4. Where can the influence of the Greeks on the Roman builders be seen? (Their influence can be seen in statues, buildings with arches, aqueducts, roads, and sewer systems.)
5. What happened to the church under the rule of Constantine? (Answers will vary. Possible answers might include that the church was strengthened, the government and church were no longer separate, and the office of the pope was created.)

Closing the Chapter

Ask students to use the outline they completed for the Note-taking activity on page 18 of this guide to summarize what they learned in the chapter.

ESL/ELL

Chapter 10: The Barbarians and the Vikings

pages 134–145

▸ Introducing the Chapter

Tapping Prior Knowledge

Ask students to preview the chapter by reading the headings and subheadings and by looking at the art and photos (on pages 134, 137, 140, and 142 of the Student Edition) and the timeline (on page 143 of the Student Edition). Then, direct students to the painting of the Vikings on page 134 of the Student Edition and the picture of the barbarian invaders attacking Rome on page 137. Ask students, *What do these images tell you about the barbarians? the Vikings? Why do you suppose that the barbarians and the Vikings had to have the qualities you named?* Encourage students to look carefully for details and to share their thoughts and observations. Ask students, *In what ways do you think the Vikings might have been different from the Romans?*

Preteaching Vocabulary

Personalizing Vocabulary Begin by asking students to preview the chapter for five unfamiliar words or phrases and to record them in their Word Logs. Once students have identified these words and phrases, ask them to use their dictionaries to define them.

Identifying Essential Vocabulary Go over the pronunciation and meaning of each word and phrase in the box below. Then, ask students to create their own sentences for each word and phrase in the box below. Ask students to rewrite their sentences, leaving a blank space for the word or phrase. Then, have students exchange sentences with another student to fill in the blanks of the other group's sentences.

Word or Phrase	Meaning
nomads	people who travel from place to place looking for food (p.135)
well-ordered	very organized (p.136)
bound to	very likely to (p.136)
mingled	to combine; to mix together (p.136)
pouring	many people coming (p.137)

▸ Applying Content Knowledge

From the Chapter: Words From the Past (page 142)

Ask students to read Words From the Past: Thor, Viking God of Thunder on page 142 of the Student Edition. Ask students to work in pairs to list five details about Thor. Then, have students research the Norse gods and list the attributes of each one. Ask students, *How are the other Norse gods similar to Thor? How are they different from Thor?*

Organizing Information

Ask students to read the section entitled Barbarian Invasions on page 137 of the Student Edition. Distribute the four-column chart on page 80 of this guide. Have students create a chart with the name of each group, who they invaded, who they were fleeing (if applicable), and where they settled.

Note-taking

Distribute the Spider Web on page 73 of this guide. Ask students to use the chapter title **The Barbarians and the Vikings** for the central topic. Then, ask students to label the spokes of their webs **The Germanic Tribes, The Barbarians, The Vikings,** and **The Normans.** Have students complete the Spider Web with key details from the chapter.

Summarizing

Direct students to the timeline on page 143 of the Student Edition. Then, distribute three copies of the Timeline on page 75 of this guide to each student. Ask students to write **Rome** at the top of the first timeline, **Europe** at the top of the second timeline, and **North America** at the top of the third timeline. Ask students to list the information from the timeline on page 143 of the Student Edition onto the appropriate timelines of their own by separating the events into three groups: Rome, Europe, and North America.

ESL/ELL

▶ Assessing Content Knowledge

Ask students to respond to the following questions. You may wish to encourage students with higher language proficiency to help beginning level students understand the questions.

Beginning Level Questions

Encourage students at this level to think about the answers to these questions and offer short verbal responses.

1. Look at page 135. What did Germanic tribes wear? (rough cloth and animal skins)
2. Look at page 137. What three things did the barbarian invaders want? (adventure, power, and riches)
3. Look at pages 139–140. Who was Charlemagne? (leader of the Franks; Emperor of the Holy Roman Empire)
4. Look at page 140. Who were the Vikings? (adventurers, sailors, and warriors from present-day Norway, Sweden, and Denmark)
5. Look at page 143. With what did the Vikings decorate buildings and ships? (carved animals)

Intermediate Level Questions

Encourage students at this level to offer verbal responses or short written responses to the following questions.

1. Look at the section entitled The Germanic Tribes. Why did the Romans believe that the Germanic tribes were uncivilized? (because they lived in tribes of nomads; dressed in animal skins; carried battle-axes; had harsh tribal laws; and were warlike)
2. Look at the section entitled Barbarian Invasions. What ended with the collapse of the Roman Empire? (fine cities; schools; study of art, science and literature; language)
3. Look at the section entitled The Franks and Charlemagne. Why was Charlemagne's empire a good one? (He built schools, encouraged artists, learned Latin, and worked with the church.)
4. Look at the section entitled Raiders From the North. What were the Northmen like? (They were adventurers who loved sailing and fighting.)
5. Look at the section entitled The Normans. What happened at the Battle of Hastings? (William killed the English king, Harold.)

Advanced Level Questions

Encourage students at this level to provide written responses in complete sentences to the following questions.

1. How were the Romans and Germans different? (Answers will vary. Possible answers might include appearance [hair and dress], lifestyle [nomadic tribes vs. stable farms and cities], education, values, and government.)
2. How did the Huns affect the Roman Empire? (They took German lands and forced the German tribes into the Roman Empire.)
3. How was the Eastern Roman Empire different from the Western? (It survived for 1,000 years after the fall of the Western Roman Empire and had fine buildings, a new university, and wealth.)
4. Why was the Battle of Hastings in 1066 important? (William, the Duke of Normandy, which is present-day France, conquered England and became the king of England.)
5. Why did people fight to conquer others? (Answers will vary. Possible answers might include land, riches, power, adventure, ruthlessness, and fear.)

▶ Closing the Chapter

Ask students to use the Spider Web that they completed for the Note-taking activity on page 20 of this guide to write a summary about what they learned.

ESL/ELL

The Lords and the Serfs

pages 146–155

Introducing the Chapter

Tapping Prior Knowledge

Ask students to preview the chapter by reading the headings and subheadings and by looking at the art and photos (on pages 146, 150, and 152 of the Student Edition) and the timeline (on page 153 of the Student Edition). Then, ask students to rewrite each of the Learning Objectives on page 146 of the Student Edition in the form of a question. For example, the first one could be rewritten as What was life like for the lord of a manor? Then, ask students which of these questions they can already answer. Encourage students to share information from their study or experience. Tell students that the questions that they are currently unable to answer they will learn the answers to as they read the chapter. Ask students, *What do you want to know about the feudal system? Life on a feudal estate? Knights?*

Preteaching Vocabulary

Personalizing Vocabulary Begin by asking students to preview the chapter for five unfamiliar words or phrases and to record them in their Word Logs. Once students have identified these words and phrases, ask them to use their dictionaries to define them.

Identifying Essential Vocabulary Go over the pronunciation and meaning of each word and phrase in the box below. Then, provide sheets of graph paper with large boxes and ask students to use the words and phrases to create a crossword puzzle. Have students use sentences from the text as the definitions. Then, have students exchange puzzles with each other to complete.

Word or Phrase	Meaning
tied to the land	not able to leave (p.147)
class	groups of people according to a social rank (p.148)
monasteries	buildings where monks live (p.150)
convents	buildings where nuns live (p.150)

Applying Content Knowledge

From the Chapter: Learn More About It (page 151)

Ask students to read Learn More About It: Knights in Armor on page 151 of the Student Edition. Then, distribute the Sequence of Events chart on page 77 of this guide. Ask students to complete the chart by writing the steps involved in becoming a knight. Ask students, *Why would someone have wanted to become a knight during medieval times?*

Note-taking

Distribute the Outline on page 76 of this guide. Write the following headings on the chalkboard and have students write them onto their outlines. As students read the chapter, ask them to use the outline to fill in the corresponding details.

```
Topic: The Feudal System
  I. Life on a Feudal Estate
     A.
     B.
     C.
 II. Men and Women of the Church
     A.
     B.
     C.
III. Knights
     A.
     B.
     C.
```

Role-playing

Ask students to write questions about information in the chapter on index cards. Then, on small pieces of paper, write **vassal, serf, freeman, knight, clergy, lord,** and **king.** Place the pieces of paper in a bag or bowl and have students choose one of the pieces of paper. Once all of the pieces of paper have been chosen, tell students that they are members of a panel and that they will answer questions or discuss issues that have been written on the index cards. Students can take turns role-playing different parts to answer the questions from the various viewpoints.

Assessing Content Knowledge

Ask students to respond to the following questions. You may wish to encourage students with higher language proficiency to help beginning level students understand the questions.

Beginning Level Questions

Encourage students at this level to think about the answers to these questions and offer short verbal responses.

1. Look at page 148. What kinds of services did the serfs provide for the lord of the manor? (grew crops; gathered wood; and took care of the lord's lands and house)
2. Look at page 150. What did men in monasteries and women in convents spend their days doing? (studying, praying, working, and taking part in religious services)
3. Look at page 151. What did knights fight to defend? (their own manors)
4. Look at page 152. What was the Black Death? (a terrible plague that caused spots of blood to turn black under the skin)
5. Look at the timeline on page 153. When did the feudal system begin? (1100 A.D.)

Intermediate Level Questions

Encourage students at this level to offer verbal responses or short written responses to the following questions.

1. Look at the section entitled The Feudal System. What was a benefit for people who lived on the manors? (Answers will vary. Possible answers might include protection, a job, and a place to live.)
2. Look at the section entitled Life on a Feudal Estate. Why was there little trade under the feudal system? (Each estate met its own needs.)
3. Look at the section entitled Life on a Feudal Estate. How did the nobles live during this time? (They lived in great houses, but with poor living conditions; they were wealthy and commanded everything on their estates; they could treat serfs as they wished.)
4. Look at the section entitled Knights. What three things did the knights fight for? (the king, their own manors, and Christianity)
5. Look at the section entitled A Hard Life. Why were knights no longer needed? (New methods of warfare were being developed.)

Advanced Level Questions

Encourage students at this level to provide written responses in complete sentences to the following questions.

1. What are four ways that life changed during the Middle Ages? (People moved from the cities to the country, towns and trade disappeared, education and learning became less important, and money was not used.)
2. How did the life of a serf differ from the life of a freeman? (Serfs lived much like slaves; they worked very hard, but owned nothing. Freemen were allowed to buy and farm their own strips of land.)
3. How was knighthood connected to Christianity? (The knights fought to protect Christianity.)
4. How might thousands of deaths from the Black Death have been prevented? (Answers will vary. Possible answers might include sanitary living conditions, inspection of people entering the country, elimination of rats, and quarantining of sick patients.)
5. Why did the feudal system begin to fade? (An increase in trade; the return of money; the movement of people back into towns; an end to the practice that awarded nobles land for services; and new methods of warfare all caused the feudal system to begin to fade.)

Closing the Chapter

Ask students to answer the questions they wrote for the Tapping Prior Knowledge activity on page 22 of this guide. Have students use the answers to their questions to write a summary about what they learned.

ESL/ELL

Chapter 12 — Islam and the Crusades
pages 156–179

▶ Introducing the Chapter

Tapping Prior Knowledge
Ask students to preview the chapter by reading the headings and subheadings and by looking at the art and photos (on pages 156, 159, 162, 163, 167, 171, and 177 of the Student Edition), the maps (on pages 161 and 165 of the Student Edition), and the timelines (on pages 162 and 176 of the Student Edition). Then, ask students to focus on the timeline entitled The Crusades on page 176 of the Student Edition. How much time passed from the beginning to the end of the Crusades? What would happen in countries that continue to fight for such a long time? Encourage students to share their thoughts about wars and the reasons for them. Ask students, *What effect might the Crusades have had on the world at that time?*

Preteaching Vocabulary
Personalizing Vocabulary Begin by asking students to preview the chapter for five unfamiliar words or phrases and to record them in their Word Logs. Once students have identified these words and phrases, ask them to use their dictionaries to define them.

Identifying Essential Vocabulary Go over the pronunciation and meaning of each word and phrase in the box below. Then, ask students to write a sentence using a word or phrase from the box below and a Word to Know from page 157 of the Student Edition.

Word or Phrase	Meaning
pilgrim	people who travel to a holy place (p.158)
force	influence or power (p.158)
flocked	to go to a place in large numbers (p.158)
persecute	to treat in a cruel way (p.160)
it was up to	depended on someone and what they decided to do (p.166)
gain the upper hand	to have more power than someone else so you have control (p.166)

▶ Applying Content Knowledge

From the Chapter: Learn More About It (page 169)
Ask students to read Learn More About It: The Ottoman Empire on page 169 of the Student Edition. Then, distribute the Who, What, Why, Where, When, and How chart on page 72 of this guide. Ask students to work with a partner to complete the chart using the information from Learn More About It.

Note-taking
Distribute the Spider Web on page 73 of this guide. Ask students to label the spokes of their webs **Muhammad and Islam, The Crusades, Medieval Towns and Cities,** and **The Magna Carta.** Have students complete their webs with key details from the chapter.

Organizing Information
Ask students to read pages 158–162 about the life of Muhammad and the Muslim religion. Then, distribute the Outline on page 76 of this guide and ask students to take notes about the life of Muhammad and the Muslim religion. Then, have students use their completed outlines to retell the story of Muhammad's life to a partner.

Personalizing the Lesson/Using Resources
Ask students to read Big Cities on page 175 of the Student Edition. Then, ask students to choose one of the cities they think they would have preferred to live in during the Middle Ages. Ask students, *Why did you choose that city?* You may wish to have students research their cities to learn what it was like in the Middle Ages and to create a brochure that would encourage tourists to come and visit.

24   Unit 4 • World History

Assessing Content Knowledge

Ask students to respond to the following questions. You may wish to encourage students with higher language proficiency to help beginning level students understand the questions.

Beginning Level Questions

Encourage students at this level to think about the answers to these questions and offer short verbal responses.

1. Look at page 158. What three groups thought Jerusalem was a holy city? (Christians, Jews, and Muslims)
2. Look at page 159. What happened to Muhammad when he was 40 years old? (He had a vision of an angel who told him to teach his people that there is one God.)
3. Look at page 163. What is the Koran? (the sacred book of Islam)
4. Look at the map on page 165. Which lands were Muslim? (Africa, Holy Land, and part of Spain)
5. Look at the timeline on page 176. Who recaptured Jerusalem in 1187 A.D.? (Saladin and Muslims)

Intermediate Level Questions

Encourage students at this level to offer verbal responses or short written responses to the following questions.

1. Look at the section entitled Christian Pilgrims. Why did people make pilgrimages? (to show their faith)
2. Look at the section entitled Muhammad and the Birth of Islam. How did many people react when Muhammad taught that there was only one God? (Most people didn't listen.)
3. Look at the section entitled The Soldiers of Christ. What was the purpose of the Crusades? (to free the Holy Land from the Turks)
4. Look at the section entitled The Holy Land Falls to the Ottomans. What did the Ottoman Turks rename their capital city Constantinople? (Istanbul)
5. Look at the section entitled Guilds. What were the guilds? (the organization of members that regulated trades and crafts)

Advanced Level Questions

Encourage students at this level to provide written responses in complete sentences to the following questions.

1. Why did the people with hard lives believe Muhammad? (He promised they would be rewarded with a wonderful life after death, which gave them hope.)
2. How did the Crusades change Europe? (Answers will vary. Possible answers might include the introduction of new foods, products, and new ideas to Europe; an increase in trade; and a sharing of cultures.)
3. Why did people prefer living in towns instead of on manors? (People had more freedom in towns than on manors.)
4. Why were the guilds important? (Answers will vary. Possible answers might include regulation, training, and opportunities for tradesmen and craftsmen.)
5. Why was the Magna Carta created? (Nobles were angry, so they drew up a list of rights that would make sure that justice would not be denied to freemen.)

Closing the Chapter

Ask students to use the Spider Webs they completed for the Note-taking activity on page 24 of this guide to write a summary about what they learned.

Chapter 13 — New Ideas: The Renaissance

pages 182–199

Introducing the Chapter

Tapping Prior Knowledge

Ask students to preview the chapter by reading the headings and subheadings and by looking at the art and photos (on pages 182, 186, 188, 193, and 194 of the Student Edition) and the timeline (on page 197 of the Student Edition). Then, direct students to the page from Leonardo da Vinci's sketchbook on page 193 of the Student Edition. Read the caption aloud. Ask students to think of the things that they use every day. Explain to students that many of those items started out as inventions. Ask students, *Why are inventions important? What effect might an inventor or an artist have on a period in history?*

Preteaching Vocabulary

Personalizing Vocabulary Begin by asking students to preview the chapter for five unfamiliar words or phrases and to record them in their Word Logs. Once students have identified these words and phrases, ask them to use their dictionaries to define them.

Identifying Essential Vocabulary Go over the pronunciation and meaning of each word and phrase in the box below. Then, distribute the Spider Web on page 73 of this guide and ask students to label the spokes **Art**, **Religion**, **Education and Learning**, and **Politics**. Ask students to fill in the web with their answers.

Word or Phrase	Meaning
ritual	ceremony always done in the same way for religious or social occasions (p.184)
lifelike	looks like a real person or thing (p.185)
hearing	a meeting of a court to find out the facts (p.191)
well rounded	someone who is able to do many different things (p.192)
movement	change or development in a situation or in attitudes (p.194)
religious orders	religious groups; societies of monks or nuns who live a holy life according to religious rules (p.196)

Applying Content Knowledge

From the Chapter: Learn More About It (page 184)

Ask students to read Learn More About It: The Humanists on page 184 of the Student Edition. Then, ask students to look at the word *humanist*. Remind students that *humanism* is a Word to Know that is listed on page 183 of the Student Edition. Tell students that it is often possible to find the meaning of a word if you know the meaning of one of its other forms. Ask students, *If* humanism *means "a concern with the needs and interests of human beings rather than religious ideas," what do you think* humanist *means?* Explain that there are other forms: *human, humanity, humane,* and *humanitarian*. For example, *human* is the word that all of the other words have in common, and it is a noun that means "a person"; *humanity* is a noun than means "people as a group"; *humane* is an adjective that means "kind or merciful"; and *humanitarian* is a noun that means "someone devoted to the welfare of people."

Note-taking

Ask students to read Education and Learning on pages 187–189 of the Student Edition. Then, have students list five results of Guttenberg's use of movable type. For example, Result 1: *Books were translated into the languages of the common people.* Result 2: *People could learn to read.* You may wish to ask students to write a paragraph that summarizes the importance of Guttenberg's use of movable type.

Personalizing the Lesson

Ask students to read The Renaissance Man on page 192. Then, distribute the Description Web of page 78 of this guide and ask students to write **The Renaissance Man** as the central topic. Then, have students list the qualities of the Renaissance man in the surrounding circles. Ask students, *Is it possible to become this kind of person today in our fast-paced, specialized world?* Have students write their opinions in a paragraph citing three to four reasons in support of their positions.

26 Unit 5 • World History

Assessing Content Knowledge

Ask students to respond to the following questions. You may wish to encourage students with higher language proficiency to help beginning level students understand the questions.

Beginning Level Questions

Encourage students at this level to think about the answers to these questions and offer short verbal responses.

1. Look at pages 189–190. What were five new inventions during this time? (Answers will vary. Possible answers include movable type, springs, watches, cast iron, the microscope, the telescope, and the pendulum.)
2. Look at page 190. What did Copernicus say about the Earth? (that it was not the center of the universe)
3. Look at page 194. What was the Reformation? (the movement that questioned the Catholic Church)
4. Look at page 196. What was the Inquisition? (a special court set up by the Roman Catholic Church to punish heretics)
5. Look at the timeline on page 197. Who are the famous men from the Renaissance? (da Vinci, Copernicus, Michelangelo, Luther, Loyola, Galileo, and Harvey)

Intermediate Level Questions

Encourage students at this level to offer verbal responses or short written responses to the following questions.

1. Look at the section entitled Michelangelo Buonarroti. What were three of Michelangelo's masterpieces? (*David*, the *Pietà*, and the ceiling of the Sistine Chapel)
2. Look at the section entitled Galileo Galilei. How did the church treat Galileo after he supported Copernicus's theory? (He was persecuted, forced to lie, and put on trial.)
3. Look at the section entitled Other Protestants. What happened on St. Bartholomew's Day? (The Catholics murdered Protestants in Paris.)
4. Look at the section entitled Other Protestants. What were some of the punishments ordered by the Inquisitions of the Roman Catholic Church? (torture, burning, and death)
5. Look at the section entitled St. Ignatius Loyola. Why did he form the Jesuit order? (to win Protestants back to the Catholic Church)

Advanced Level Questions

Encourage students at this level to provide written responses in complete sentences to the following questions.

1. What were the Humanists' criticisms of the church? (They believed that the church was too concerned with wealth and power and that there was too much ritual and ceremony in the church.)
2. Why do you think Galileo's ideas about the planets were so controversial? (Answers will vary. Possible answers might include the fact that it changed hundreds of years of thought; it reduced the Earth to just another planet, not the center of the universe, it also might have meant that other ideas were wrong; and it questioned the authority of the church.)
3. Why do you think that most people did not believe Copernicus? (Answers will vary. Possible answers might include that he questioned church practices, challenged the authority of the pope, and refused to take back what he had said.)
4. Why did Leonardo da Vinci have such a big impact in the Renaissance? (He invented many new things and created many beautiful works of art that defined the Renaissance.)
5. What was the Counter Reformation? (It was a movement for change within the Catholic Church.)

Closing the Chapter

Distribute the Outline on page 76 of this guide. Ask students to complete the outline using the section headings and key details from the chapter. Then, have students use their outlines to write a summary about what they learned.

ESL/ELL

Kings and Queens

pages 200–213

Introducing the Chapter

Tapping Prior Knowledge
Ask students to preview the chapter by reading the headings and subheadings and by looking at the art and photos (on pages 200, 205, 207, 208, and 210 of the Student Edition) and the timelines (on pages 209 and 211 of the Student Edition). Then, ask students to rewrite each of the Learning Objectives on page 200 of the Student Edition in the form of a question. For example, the first one could be rewritten as What was King Philip II of Spain's goal? Then, ask students which of these questions they can already answer. Tell students that they will learn the answers to the questions that they are currently unable to answer as they read the chapter. Ask students, *Why might kings and queens have had an important role in Europe during this time?*

Preteaching Vocabulary
Personalizing Vocabulary Begin by asking students to preview the chapter for five unfamiliar words or phrases and to record them in their Word Logs. Once students have identified these words and phrases, ask them to use their dictionaries to define them.

Identifying Essential Vocabulary Go over the pronunciation and meaning of each word and phrase in the box below. Then, ask students to classify each of the following phrases as a noun (n.), noun phrase (n.p.), a verb (v.), or a verb phrase (v.p.).

Word or Phrase	Meaning
unified (v.)	connected (p.201)
nation-state (n.p.)	a politically independent country (p.201)
bond (n.)	a special relationship with someone or something (p.201)
assassinated (v.)	murdered an important person (p.206)
in an uproar (v.p.)	angry protest (p.206)
beheaded (v.)	cut off someone's head as a punishment (p.208)
outlived (v.)	lived longer than someone else (p.208)

Applying Content Knowledge

From the Chapter: Learn More About It (page 204)
Ask students to read Learn More About It: The Spanish Armada on page 204 of the Student Edition. Then, distribute the Sequence of Events chart on page 77 of this guide. Have students work with a partner to sequence the events that led to the defeat of the Spanish Armada. Students may wish to include details under each event as they create their charts.

Organizing Information
Distribute the four-column chart on page 80 of this guide. Ask students to label the columns of their charts **Monarch (Years Ruled)**, **Religion**, **Accomplishments**, and **Failures**. Have students complete their charts using key details from the chapter.

Using Resources
Distribute the Who, What, Why, Where, When, and How chart on page 72 of this guide. Have students write **Who is the person I chose?** under **Who** in the chart; **What did _____ do?** under **What** in the chart; **Why was _____ important?** under **Why** in the chart; **Where did _____ have the greatest impact?** under **Where** in the chart; **When did _____ have the greatest impact?** under **When** in the chart; and **How did _____ have the greatest impact?** under **How** in the chart. Students may use these questions or create their own. Ask students to work in pairs to complete their charts by researching the life of one of the wives or children of Henry VIII. Ask students to prepare a short written report of their research. Encourage students to use copies of illustrations that they find in books or on the Internet in their written reports. When students have completed their research, put all of their reports in a class biography book called *King Henry's Wives and Children*.

Assessing Content Knowledge

Ask students to respond to the following questions. You may wish to encourage students with higher language proficiency to help beginning level students understand the questions.

Beginning Level Questions

Encourage students at this level to think about the answers to these questions and offer short verbal responses.

1. Look at page 201. Which three countries became unified into nation-states? (Spain, France, and England)
2. Look at page 204. What was the Spanish Armada? (a large fleet of Spanish ships)
3. Look at page 207. Why didn't Henry want to be married to Catherine of Aragon? (Catherine was only able to have a girl, and Henry wanted a boy.)
4. Look at the timeline on page 209. How many monarchs ruled Europe during this time? (seven)
5. Look at the timeline on page 211. In what year did the Dutch revolt against Spain begin? (1568)

Intermediate Level Questions

Encourage students at this level to offer verbal responses or short written responses to the following questions.

1. Look at the section entitled The Age of the Monarchs. What were the two powerful forces that shaped sixteenth-century European history? (nationalism and religious beliefs)
2. Look at the section entitled Spain. Why were many Jews and Moors tortured and killed in Spain in the late 1400s? (King Ferdinand and Queen Isabella called upon the Inquisition to hunt down anyone who was not Catholic. They did not want anyone except Roman Catholics in Spain.)
3. Look at the section entitled King Philip and the Netherlands. What happened in the Netherlands when King Philip II demanded that its people be Catholic? (The Dutch rebelled and declared their independence.)
4. Look at the section entitled "Good King Henry." What did Henry IV of France have to do in order to be king? (He had to agree to be a Catholic.)
5. Look at the section entitled Elizabeth's England. Who were three great writers during Queen Elizabeth's reign? (Shakespeare, Spencer, and Bacon)

Advanced Level Questions

Encourage students at this level to provide written responses in complete sentences to the following questions.

1. Why did Queen Elizabeth of England oppose King Philip of Spain? (She was Protestant, and he wanted all of Europe to be Catholic.)
2. What did Queen Elizabeth I do to get in the way of Philip II's plan to make all of Europe Catholic? (She helped the Netherlands, and she gave English ships permission to attack Spanish ships.)
3. What might have happened in Europe if the Spanish Armada had defeated the English? (Answers will vary. Possible answers might include Spain's power over England, strengthening of Catholicism, the decline of England instead of the Elizabethan Age.)
4. What did Queen Mary I do to try to make England Roman Catholic? (She struck down laws supporting the Protestants; she made new laws enforcing Catholicism; she had more than 300 Protestants burned to death; and she tried to make Catholicism the state religion.)
5. Why might Queen Elizabeth have allowed sailors to explore the world in her name? (Answers will vary.)

Closing the Chapter

Ask students to answer the questions they wrote for the Tapping Prior Knowledge activity on page 28 of this guide. Have students use the answers to their questions to write a summary about what they learned.

ESL/ELL

Chapter 15: To the East; To the West

pages 216–235

Introducing the Chapter

Tapping Prior Knowledge
Ask students to preview the chapter by reading the headings and subheadings and by looking at the art and photos (on pages 216, 220, 222, 224, and 232 of the Student Edition), the map (on page 228 of the Student Edition), and the timeline (on page 233 of the Student Edition). Then, ask students, *What are some of the major differences in the Eastern and Western traditions and cultures?* Encourage students to talk about their knowledge of Eastern and Western cultures from prior study or personal experience. Ask students, *How might it be possible for cultures to develop in different ways?*

Preteaching Vocabulary

Personalizing Vocabulary Begin by asking students to preview the chapter for five unfamiliar words or phrases and to record them in their Word Logs. Once students have identified these words and phrases, ask them to use their dictionaries to define them.

Identifying Essential Vocabulary Go over the pronunciation and meaning of each word in the box below. Then, distribute an index card to each student. Ask each student to write a question on the index card using one or more of the vocabulary words. Then, have students select a partner to exchange cards with and have each student answer their partner's question.

Word or Phrase	Meaning
actual	real (p.217)
destined	will happen in the future (p.218)
clever	able to use your intelligence to do something (p.218)
thrived	became very successful or very strong and healthy (p.221)
mound	a pile of dirt, sand, or stones that looks like a small hill (p.227)
tributes	payment of goods or money by one ruler to a more powerful ruler (p.230)
legend	an old story that cannot be proven (p.231)

Applying Content Knowledge

From the Chapter: Great Names in History (page 219)
Ask students to read Great Names in History: Kublai Khan on page 219 of the Student Edition. Then, ask pairs of students to write eight facts about Kublai Khan. Ask students, *What kind of a leader was Kublai Khan?* Ask students to arrive at a conclusion about Kublai Kahn's leadership and write a paragraph that summarizes their conclusions.

Using Resources
Ask students to study the photograph of the Taj Mahal on page 216 of the Student Edition. Ask students, *What kinds of details can you observe from the photo?* Ask groups of students to list details that they can observe from the photo. Distribute the Who, What, Why, Where, When, and How chart on page 72 of this guide. Have students write **Who built the Taj Mahal?** under **Who** in the chart; **What is the Taj Mahal?** under **What** in the chart; **Why is the Taj Mahal important?** under **Why** in the chart; **Where is the Taj Mahal?** under **Where** in the chart; **When was the Taj Mahal built?** under **When** in the chart; and **How was the Taj Mahal built?** under **How** in the chart. Students may use these questions or create their own. Then, ask students to research the Taj Mahal in books or on the Internet and use the details they find to complete their charts. Once students have completed their Who, What, Why, Where, When, and How charts, ask them to use their charts to write a summary about what they learned about the Taj Mahal.

Using Visuals
Distribute the Spider Web on page 73 of this guide. As students study the chapter, have them record each new culture on a spoke of the web and the details for that culture in the corresponding section. Then, have students use their completed webs to create a poster for the cultures. Ask students, *In what ways are these cultures the same? In what ways are these cultures different?*

Assessing Content Knowledge

Ask students to respond to the following questions. You may wish to encourage students with higher language proficiency to help beginning level students understand the questions.

Beginning Level Questions

Encourage students at this level to think about the answers to these questions and offer short verbal responses.

1. Look at page 218. What was the Silk Road? (a route between China and Europe)
2. Look at page 221. Why is little known about the early history of Japan? (The ancient Japanese had no system of writing.)
3. Look at page 226. Where did the first Muslims come from? (Arabia)
4. Look at the map on page 228. What gulf is shown on the map? (the Gulf of Mexico)
5. Look at the timeline on page 233. What happened in A.D. 1368 ? (The Mongol rulers were overthrown, and the Ming Dynasty began in China.)

Intermediate Level Questions

Encourage students at this level to offer verbal responses or short written responses to the following questions.

1. Look at the section entitled In China… .What was the result of China's isolation? (There was little change in Chinese culture.)
2. Look at the section entitled The Hermit Nation. Why could Japan have been called a hermit nation? (Japan showed little interest in the rest of the world and remained isolated like China.)
3. Look at the section entitled The Moguls Invade India… .Why was Akbar the greatest Mogul emperor? (He was a wise ruler; he was a Muslim, but he let others worship as they pleased; and he tried to bring people of all religions together to live in harmony.)
4. Look at the section entitled The Aztecs. Why didn't the Aztecs need money? (They bartered for goods.)
5. Look at the timeline on page 233. What events occurred in Asia and the Americas in the sixteenth century? (Cortéz came to Tenochtitlán; Moguls invaded India; Pizarro came to South America; it was the end of the Inca Empire.)

Advanced Level Questions

Encourage students at this level to provide written responses in complete sentences to the following questions.

1. What did Marco Polo learn about China? (Answers will vary. Students' answers might include information about the Chinese civilization, their advances in knowledge and inventions, and the ease of travel.)
2. What were the positives and negatives of Japanese isolation for Japan? (Positives: Other influences were kept out of Japan; the Japanese were able to maintain their culture; isolation limited disease; and they were not conquered. Negatives: Knowledge of other cultures was limited; advancements made in other cultures would not be shared with the Japanese; and the feudal system stayed in power.)
3. Why did most of India's people turn to the teachings of Buddha? (Many of India's people turned to the teachings of Buddha because they turned away from the Hindu religion and its strict caste laws.)
4. How did each of the Native American civilizations in North America live? (Answers will vary. Possible answers should reflect an awareness of how location determined lifestyles.)
5. Why are roads in a giant empire so important? (Answers will vary. Possible answers might include ideas of communication, transportation, and the goal of connecting all parts of the empire.)

Closing the Chapter

Ask students to use the Spider Web and the poster they completed for the Using Visuals activity on page 30 of this guide to write a summary about what they learned.

Chapter 16: Explorers, Traders, and Settlers
pages 236–247

▶ Introducing the Chapter

Tapping Prior Knowledge
Ask students to preview the chapter by reading the headings and subheadings and by looking at the art and photos (on pages 236 and 240 of the Student Edition), the maps (on pages 238 and 243 of the Student Edition), and the timeline (on page 245 of the Student Edition). Then, ask students if they have ever explored something. Ask students, *What was it? What caused you to explore it?* Encourage students to share their stories and personal experiences. Then, ask students, *What is the purpose of exploring something?* Students should understand that exploration can happen, for example, out of need or out of curiosity. Ask students, *Why might explorers have been important during the course of history?*

Preteaching Vocabulary

Personalizing Vocabulary Begin by asking students to preview the chapter for five unfamiliar words or phrases and to record them in their Word Logs. Once students have identified these words and phrases, ask them to use their dictionaries to define them.

Identifying Essential Vocabulary Go over the pronunciation and meaning of each word in the box below. Then, distribute the four-column chart on page 80 of this guide. Have students create a chart using the following headings: **Word, Sentence From the Text, Synonym,** and **My Sentence.**

Word or Phrase	Meaning
route	a way to go from one place to another (p.237)
cartographer	someone who makes maps (p.238)
proof	facts, information, and documents that show that something is true (p.239)
suffer	to experience physical or mental pain (p.240)
driven	to force someone to leave an area (p.243)
ventures	new business activites that involve taking risks (p.245)

▶ Applying Content Knowledge

From the Chapter: History Fact (page 244)
Ask students to read the History Fact on page 244 of the Student Edition. Then, bring to class copies of the business section from a newspaper that shows stock prices. Explain to students that many companies today offer shares of stock just like the trading companies did in the 1600s. Then, ask students to choose a stock that they could follow for the rest of the school year. You may wish to have students record their stocks' progress on a daily or a weekly basis and create a graph at the end of the year that shows the stocks' progress.

Using Visuals
Ask students to review pages 237–239 of the Student Edition. Then, distribute the Idea Web on page 81 of this guide. Have students write the name of each explorer in one of the sections and record key details about each of the explorers. Then, have students create newspaper articles that describe each explorer and his expedition. Students' articles should include the name of the explorer, the year of the exploration, and where he sailed, as well as any other interesting and important details that they recorded in their webs. Encourage students to be as creative as they would like to be. You may wish to paste students' completed articles onto an 11-x-17-inch sheet of paper and have students create a masthead to paste to the top of the 11-x-17-inch sheet of paper.

Role-playing
Have students write one or two questions about something they learned in the chapter. Then, on small pieces of paper, write the names of each of the explorers, traders, and settlers. Place the pieces of paper into a box and ask students to choose one. Have students ask the questions they wrote and answer the questions from the viewpoint of the person they chose.

Organizing Information
Distribute the Outline on page 76 of this guide. As students read the chapter, ask them to complete the outline using the headings and details from the chapter.

Assessing Content Knowledge

Ask students to respond to the following questions. You may wish to encourage students with higher language proficiency to help beginning level students understand the questions.

Beginning Level Questions

Encourage students at this level to think about the answers to these questions and offer short verbal responses.

1. Look at page 237. What was Columbus looking for? (a water route to Asia)
2. Look at the map on page 238. Who were the explorers? (Cabot, Cabral, Columbus, Da Gama, and Magellan)
3. Look at page 241. What countries participated in the slave trade? (Spain, Portugal, England, and France)
4. Look at page 244. How did merchants help pay for sea voyages? (by offering shares of stock)
5. Look at the timeline on page 245. What are three countries that explored the Americas? (Portugal, France, and England)

Intermediate Level Questions

Encourage students at this level to offer verbal responses or short written responses to the following questions.

1. Look at the sections entitled Christopher Columbus and Portuguese Explorers. Where did each of the explorers travel? (Columbus – West Indies; Da Gama – Cape of Good Hope to India; Cabral – Brazil; Magellan – around the world.)
2. Look at the section entitled Settlers. Why did the Europeans come to North America? (They wanted religious freedom, a better life, and adventure.)
3. Look at the section entitled Settlers. What did the Europeans bring to the Native Americans? (new ways, new religions, and new diseases)
4. Look at the section entitled Traders. What happened by 1763 in the French and Indian War? (The English had taken all of Canada from the French.)
5. Look at the section entitled The New Middle Class. Why did successful trade ventures result in a new middle class? (European merchants became wealthy.)

Advanced Level Questions

Encourage students at this level to provide written responses in complete sentences to the following questions.

1. Do you think the three ships Queen Isabella and King Ferdinand gave Columbus were a good investment of their money? Explain your answer. (Answers will vary. Possible answers should mention the land and wealth that Spain acquired because of this voyage.)
2. Columbus wanted to sail west to find a shorter route from Europe to Asia. What do you think Columbus believed about the size of the world? (Columbus probably thought it was much smaller than it actually is.)
3. How did Spain create an empire by A.D. 1600? (Spain claimed present-day Mexico, Florida, Central America, the Caribbean Islands, and South America.)
4. What land did the French trappers claim? (The French trappers claimed land along the Mississippi River and in Canada.)
5. Why were banks important to trading companies? (Banks helped pay for trading ships.)

Closing the Chapter

Ask students to use the outlines they completed for the Organizing Information activity on page 32 of this guide to write a summary about what they learned.

ESL/ELL

Chapter 17: The Struggle for Democracy

pages 250–261

▶ Introducing the Chapter

Tapping Prior Knowledge

Ask students to preview the chapter by reading the headings and subheadings and by looking at the art and photos (on pages 250, 255, 256, and 259 of the Student Edition) and the timeline (on page 258 of the Student Edition). Ask students what the word *revolution* means. Encourage students to use their bilingual dictionaries to define the word. Have students suggest possible meanings of the word and work with students to arrive at a clear explanation of the word. Then, ask students, *What changes might happen because of a revolution?*

Preteaching Vocabulary

Personalizing Vocabulary Begin by asking students to preview the chapter for five unfamiliar words or phrases and to record them in their Word Logs. Once students have identified these words and phrases, ask them to use their dictionaries to define them.

Identifying Essential Vocabulary Go over the pronunciation and meaning of each word and phrase in the box below. Then, distribute the four-column chart on page 80 of this guide. Ask students to work with a partner to find the phrases in the box below as they are used in the text. Have the students create a chart using the following headings: **Word or Phrase, Meaning Clues From the Text, Definition,** and **My Sentence.**

Word or Phrase	Meaning
reason	think, understand, and form judgments that are based on fact (p.251)
granted	gave people something they have asked for, especially official permission (p.252)
absolute power	complete power with no limit (p.253)
keep his word	do what you have promised (p.254)
to put reins on	to control (p.254)

▶ Applying Content Knowledge

From the Chapter: Words From the Past (page 259)

Ask students to read Words From the Past: The Declaration of Independence on page 259 of the Student Edition. You might wish to read aloud the passages quoted from the document. Then, ask students to work in small groups and have each group research a famous document. Distribute the Who, What, Why, Where, When, and How chart on page 72 of this guide. Have students write **Who wrote (the name of the document)?** under **Who** in the chart; **What is the purpose of (the name of the document)?** under **What** in the chart; **Why is (the name of the document) important?** under **Why** in the chart; **Where did (the name of the document) have the greatest impact?** under **Where** in the chart; **When was (the name of the document) created?** under **When** in the chart; and **How did (the name of the document) affect the people at the time?** under **How** in the chart. Students might wish to make a poster entitled Documents That Changed theWorld, listing each document and the change it created.

Organizing Information

Ask students to read King Charles I Does Away With Parliament and Civil War in England on pages 253–254 of the Student Edition. Have students take notes on the steps that led up to the English Civil War. Then, distribute the Sequence of Events chart on page 77 of this guide and ask students to organize the steps that led up to the English Civil War. Then, have students use their charts to write a summary.

Personalizing the Lesson

Distribute the Description Web on page 78 of this guide. Ask students to write the name of an important man or woman from their countries or cultures in the center shape. Then, have students write details that describe the person and his or her contributions to the culture in the surrounding shapes. Ask students to use their webs to develop a paragraph about the important man or woman from their countries or cultures that they chose and his or her contributions to that culture.

Assessing Content Knowledge

Ask students to respond to the following questions. You may wish to encourage students with higher language proficiency to help beginning level students understand the questions.

Beginning Level Questions

Encourage students at this level to think about the answers to these questions and offer short verbal responses.

1. Look at page 251. What three things did philosophers believe? (See page 251.)
2. Look at page 253. During what years did King Charles I rule England? (from 1625 to 1649)
3. Look at pages 257. What document served as the model for the American Bill of Rights? (the British Bill of Rights)
4. Look at the timeline on page 258. How many years passed between the English Bill of Rights and the American Declaration of Independence? (87 years)
5. Look at page 259. According to the Declaration of Independence, where does government get its power? (from the consent of the governed)

Intermediate Level Questions

Encourage students at this level to offer verbal responses or short written responses to the following questions.

1. Look at the sections entitled The Road to Revolution in England and Parliament. How was Parliament created? (The Great Council was expanded by Edward I to include merchants, knights, and landowners.)
2. Look at the section entitled Civil War in England. Why did the Puritans disagree with King Charles? (They disagreed with King Charles about the church and other matters.)
3. Look at the section entitled The Glorious Revolution. How were William and Mary different from other English monarchs? (They understood the importance of democracy.)
4. Look at the section entitled Revolution in America. What were the complaints of the American colonists? (The king demanded high taxes from the colonists, but the colonists had no say in the government.)
5. Look at the section entitled Revolution in America. What did the colonists want from the king? (Some wanted rights; others wanted freedom.)

Advanced Level Questions

Encourage students at this level to provide written responses in complete sentences to the following questions.

1. Read the quotes on page 251. Why do you think these ideas led to revolution? (Answers will vary. Possible answers might reflect beliefs in the power of the individual man and questions about the power of kings, particularly the divine right of kings.)
2. What ideas from the Age of Reason began to change government and society? (Answers will vary. Possible answers might include ideas of natural rights, freedom, questioning the divine right of kings, and the ability of all men to reason and question.)
3. What important change did the Bill of Rights make in English government? (It stated that the monarch could act only after consulting Parliament, which made Parliament a strong force in the government.)
4. Why was the American Revolution important to other countries? (It gave hope to people that they could have freedom.)
5. How are the ideas in the Declaration of Independence different from the ideas about government in the past? (In the past, people believed that the king received his right to govern from God and that people had no voice in government.)

Closing the Chapter

Ask students to rewrite each heading in the chapter in the form of a question. For example, the section entitled The Road to Revolution in England could be rewritten as What led to the Road to Revolution in England? and the section entitled Parliament could be rewritten as What is Parliament? or Why was Parliament important? Once students have rewritten each heading in the form of a question, have students write answers for each of the questions.

ESL/ELL

Revolution in France

pages 262–277

Introducing the Chapter

Tapping Prior Knowledge

Ask students to preview the chapter by reading the headings and subheadings and by looking at the art and photos (on pages 262, 264, 265, 269, 270, and 272 of the Student Edition), the map (on page 271 of the Student Edition), and the timeline (on page 275 of the Student Edition). Ask students to recall the definition for the word *revolution* that they arrived at for the Tapping Prior Knowledge activity on page 34 of this guide. Then, direct students to the art on page 262 of the Student Edition. Ask students, *What information about the revolution can you gather from this painting of the French Revolution?* Write students' observations on the chalkboard. Ask students, *How might the French Revolution have put the country into chaos?*

Preteaching Vocabulary

Personalizing Vocabulary Begin by asking students to preview the chapter for five unfamiliar words or phrases and to record them in their Word Logs. Once students have identified these words and phrases, ask them to use their dictionaries to define them.

Identifying Essential Vocabulary Go over the pronunciation and meaning of each word and phrase in the box below. Then, ask students to combine one of these words or phrases with a vocabulary word from the list of Words to Know on page 263 of the Student Edition to create a sentence.

Word or Phrase	Meaning
locked into	not able to change (p.263)
brewing	something that will happen soon (p.264)
storm	attack (p.266)
boiling point	a point when people cannot deal calmly with a situation anymore (p.266)
alarmed	worried and frightened (p.266)
corrupt	dishonest, illegal, or immoral (p.270)
took heart	became encouraged (p.273)

Applying Content Knowledge

From the Chapter: Learn More About It (page 273)

Ask students to read Learn More About It: Napoleon's Mistake on page 273 of the Student Edition. First, distribute the Who, What, Why, Where, When, and How chart on page 72 of this guide. Have students write **Who was Napoleon Bonaparte?** under **Who** in the chart; **What was Napoleon's mistake?** under **What** in the chart; **Why was it a mistake?** under **Why** in the chart; **Where did the mistake happen?** under **Where** in the chart; **When did the mistake happen?** under **When** in the chart; and **How did the mistake affect the outcome of the war?** under **How** in the chart. Students may use these questions or create their own. Second, distribute the Sequence of Events chart on page 77 of this guide and ask students to list the steps in Napoleon's defeat in Russia.

Organizing Information

Ask students to read pages 264–266 of the Student Edition. Have students take notes on the steps that led up to the storming of the Bastille. Then, distribute the Sequence of Events chart on page 77 of this guide and ask students to organize the steps that led up to the storming of the Bastille. Ask students to use their charts to write a summary.

Summarizing

Distribute the Outline on page 76 of this guide. As students read the chapter, ask them to use the outline to fill in the headings and corresponding details.

> Topic: Napoleon's Influence on France
> I. France Before Napoleon
>   A.
>   B.
> II. France Under Napoleon
>   A.
>   B.
> III. France After Napoleon
>   A.
>   B.

36 Unit 7 • World History

ESL/ELL

Assessing Content Knowledge

Ask students to respond to the following questions. You may wish to encourage students with higher language proficiency to help beginning level students understand the questions.

Beginning Level Questions

Encourage students at this level to think about the answers to these questions and offer short verbal responses.

1. Look at page 264. What was the Estates-General? (a government body like Britain's Parliament)
2. Look at page 266. What was the Bastille? (a dark, mysterious place where people were locked away for disagreeing with the king or for failing to pay taxes)
3. Look at the map on page 271. Which lands did France control? (See page 271.)
4. Look at page 274. Who defeated Napoleon at Waterloo? (the Duke of Wellington with troops from Britain, Belgium, Hanover, the Netherlands, and Prussia)
5. Look at the timeline on page 275. How many republics were there? (three republics)

Intermediate Level Questions

Encourage students at this level to offer verbal responses or short written responses to the following questions.

1. Look at the section entitled The Age of Reason. Why was life in France in the 1700s unfair? (Nobles lived splendidly; peasants often went hungry)
2. Look at the section entitled The Age of Reason. Why had the French helped the Americans in their war for independence? (The nobles wanted to see the British defeated; the peasants wanted to fight against tyranny.)
3. Look at the section entitled The French Revolution. What was the purpose of the new constitution that was written by the National Assembly? (It included new laws that did away with the feudal system.)
4. Look at the section entitled The Reign of Terror. Why wasn't Robespierre a successful leader? (Answers will vary.)
5. Look at the section entitled Napoleon Bonaparte. What event started Napoleon's rise to power? (He put down an uprising by 30,000 national guardsmen.)

Advanced Level Questions

Encourage students at this level to provide written responses in complete sentences to the following questions.

1. Why do you think the peasants accepted their poor fate? (Answers will vary. Possible answers might include ideas about people believing that their place in life was determined by God or that kings ruled by divine right, so everyone had to accept it.)
2. Who were the estates, and why was their representation unfair? (The first consisted of wealthy clergy, the second were the nobles, and the third was the middle class and peasants. It was unfair because each estate had one vote, although the Third Estate represented 98 percent of the population. The nobility and clergy could vote together and control decisions.)
3. What event turned the revolutionaries against Louis XVI? (The armies from Austria and Prussia that came to crush the revolution turned the revolutionaries against Louis XVI.)
4. What do you think would have happened to Louis XVI if the rulers of Austria and Prussia had not sent armies? (Answers will vary. Accept all reasonable responses.)
5. What did Napoleon do to take control of France? (He won battles, he pushed out the Directory, he put himself directly in charge of the army, and he set up a police force responsible only to him.)

Closing the Chapter

Ask students to use the outlines they completed for the Summarizing activity on page 36 of this guide to write a summary about what they learned.

ESL/ELL

Chapter 19: The Industrial Revolution

pages 280–293

▶ Introducing the Chapter

Tapping Prior Knowledge
Ask students to preview the chapter by reading the headings and subheadings and by looking at the art and photos (on pages 280, 284, 286, 288, and 290 of the Student Edition) and the timeline (on page 291 of the Student Edition). Ask students what the phrase *Industrial Revolution* means. Encourage students to recall when they have seen the word *revolution* used in earlier chapters. Then, ask students, *What kind of revolution do you think the Industrial Revolution was?*

Preteaching Vocabulary
Personalizing Vocabulary Begin by asking students to preview the chapter for five unfamiliar words or phrases and to record them in their Word Logs. Once students have identified these words and phrases, ask them to use their dictionaries to define them.

Identifying Essential Vocabulary Go over the pronunciation and meaning of each word and phrase in the box below. Then, provide sheets of graph paper with large boxes and ask students to use the words and phrases to create a crossword puzzle. Have students use sentences from the text as the definitions. Then, have students exchange puzzles with each other and complete them.

Word or Phrase	Meaning
make a profit	gain money from doing business (p.282)
spun	made cotton or wool into thread (p.283)
spare time	time when you are not working (p.283)
yarn	thread made of cotton or wool (p.284)
factory hands	people who work in factories (p.284)
weavers	someone who weaves cloth (p.285)
spinners	someone who makes thread (p.285)
loom	a frame or machine used to weave thread into cloth (p.285)
imperialism	conquering, forming colonies, or controlling the government and wealth of weaker lands (p.287)

▶ Applying Content Knowledge

From the Chapter: History Fact (page 285)
Ask students to read the History Fact on page 285 of the Student Edition. Explain to students that adding *–ites* to the end of a word identifies a person as part of a group. Therefore, a *luddite* is someone who belongs to the group of workers who destroyed machines in the early 1800s. Tell students that other examples of this include *Moabite*, which means "a person from Moab"; *Yemenite,* which means "a person from Yemen"; and *Israelite,* which means "a person from Israel." Ask students, *Why is it useful to know the meaning of an ending that can be added to a word to change its meaning?*

Note-taking
Ask students to read Great Britain Leads the Industrial Revolution on page 282. Then, distribute the Idea Web on page 81 of this guide and ask students to work with a partner and write the main idea in the central shape. Then, have students find one important sentence and two details in each paragraph for the outer shapes of the web. The fifth paragraph is short, so it will have no details.

Using Resources
Ask students to read pages 283–286 of the Student Edition. Then, ask students to work in small groups and have each group research one of the inventions. Distribute the Who, What, Why, Where, When, and How chart on page 72 of this guide. Have students write **Who invented (the name of the invention)?** under **Who** in the chart; **What is the purpose of (the name of the invention)?** under **What** in the chart; **Why was (the name of the invention) invented?** under **Why** in the chart; **Where was (the name of the invention) used?** under **Where** in the chart; **When was (the name of the invention) invented?** under **When** in the chart; and **How did (the name of the invention) affect the lives of the people who used it?** under **How** in the chart. Students may use these questions or create their own. Students might wish to make a poster entitled Inventions, listing each invention and the impact it had.

ESL/ELL

Assessing Content Knowledge

Ask students to respond to the following questions. You may wish to encourage students with higher language proficiency to help beginning level students understand the questions.

Beginning Level Questions

Encourage students at this level to think about the answers to these questions and offer short verbal responses.

1. Look at page 282. What countries make up Great Britain? (England, Scotland, and Wales)
2. Look at page 283. What did Britain's textile industry produce? (cloth)
3. Look at page 287. How were workers' lives improved? (Incomes increased, food improved, and heating and cooking improved.)
4. Look at pages 289–290. What were living conditions in the cities like during the Industrial Revolution? (polluted, crowded, lacked sanitary conditions, housed disease)
5. Look at the timeline on page 291. What inventions were created during the eighteenth century? (See page 291.)

Intermediate Level Questions

Encourage students at this level to offer verbal responses or short written responses to the following questions.

1. Look at the sections entitled The Textile Industry and New Inventions Move Textile-Making Out of Cottages. What was the difference between a cottage industry and big business? (Cottage industries are small at-home operations; big business employs people to work in factories.)
2. Look at the section entitled Electricity and Petroleum. Why was the discovery of petroleum important? (It could be used for many things, and there was a good supply of it available in the United States.)
3. Look at the section entitled Imperialism. How did imperialism solve the problem of getting raw materials? (Colonies were sources of raw materials.)
4. Look at the section entitled The Industrial Revolution Changes Life: The Cities. Why did people begin to protest? (They disagreed with employing young children, the low wages, and the lack of safety.)
5. Look at the section entitled The Industrial Revolution Changes Life: The Cities. Why do you think factory owners were against labor unions? (Answers will vary.)

Advanced Level Questions

Encourage students at this level to provide written responses in complete sentences to the following questions.

1. Why do you think people wanted to destroy the machines? (People feared losing their jobs.)
2. How did the steam engine change transportation? (It led to the development of the steam locomotive and the river steamboat.)
3. How did children help factory owners save money? (Children worked for lower wages.)
4. What are the positive and negative results of the Industrial Revolution? (Positive: It made life better for many people; people had better food to eat; people had coal to heat their homes and cook their food; businessmen became wealthy; new inventions in communication let people learn what was going on in their world. Negative: Life got harder for many city workers because they spent long days in dirty, dangerous factories, working for poor wages.)
5. How did countries become dependent on each other as a result of the Industrial Revolution? (Countries had to work out trade agreements; they needed other countries for raw materials.)

Closing the Chapter

Ask small groups of students to summarize the most important points from the chapter and then list (1) the changes that occurred during the Industrial Revolution, (2) the effects the changes had on the world, and (3) the effects the changes had on the lives of the people. Ask students to use the important points they identified to write a summary about what they learned.

ESL/ELL

Chapter 20: Independence in Latin America

pages 294–305

▶ Introducing the Chapter

Tapping Prior Knowledge

Ask students to preview the chapter by reading the headings and subheadings and by looking at the art and photos (on pages 294, 297, and 303 of the Student Edition), the map (on page 302 of the Student Edition), and the timeline (on page 303 of the Student Edition). Then, ask students what the words *independent* and *dependent* mean. Encourage students to use their bilingual dictionaries to define the words. Have students suggest possible meanings of each word and work with students to arrive at a clear explanation of the word. Then, ask students, *What does it mean to be dependent? What does it mean to be independent? What qualities does an independent person have?* Ask students, *Why would a country want to win independence from another country?*

Preteaching Vocabulary

Personalizing Vocabulary Begin by asking students to preview the chapter for five unfamiliar words or phrases and to record them in their Word Logs. Once students have identified these words and phrases, ask them to use their dictionaries to define them.

Identifying Essential Vocabulary Go over the pronunciation and meaning of each word and phrase in the box below. Then, distribute the four-column chart on page 80 of this guide. Have students create a chart using the following headings: **Word or Phrase**, **Meaning Clues From the Text**, **Definition**, and **My Sentence**.

▶ Applying Content Knowledge

From the Chapter: Great Names in History (page 300)

Ask students to read Great Names in History: José de San Martín on page 300 of the Student Edition. First, distribute the Who, What, Why, Where, When, and How chart on page 72 of this guide. Have students write **Who was José de San Martín?** under **Who** in the chart; **What did José de San Martín do?** under **What** in the chart; **Why did José de San Martín do what he did?** under **Why** in the chart; **Where did José de San Martín do what he did?** under **Where** in the chart; **When did José de San Martín do what he did?** under **When** in the chart; and **How did José de San Martín's actions affect history?** under **How** in the chart. Students may use these questions or create their own. Second, distribute the Sequence of Events chart on page 77 of this guide and ask students to sequence the events in San Martín's life.

Using Visuals

Ask students to study the map entitled Latin American Nations Become Independent on page 302 of the Student Edition. Distribute the Timeline on page 75 of this guide and ask students to complete the timeline according to the year each country became independent.

Organizing Information

Distribute the Outline on page 76 of this guide. As students read the chapter, ask them to complete the outline with key details from the chapter about the six Latin American revolutionaries. Suggest that students include the countries that each of the revolutionaries liberated, the date of liberation, and the personal outcome for each of the revolutionaries.

Word or Phrase	Meaning
field hands	people who work on farms (p.296)
dependent	needing someone or something else to exist, to be successful, and to be healthy (p.296)
crushed	completely defeated (p.296)
haughty	proud and unfriendly opinions and feelings (p.296)
backing	supporting or helping, especially with money (p.298)

Unit 8 • World History

Assessing Content Knowledge

Ask students to respond to the following questions. You may wish to encourage students with higher language proficiency to help beginning level students understand the questions.

Beginning Level Questions

Encourage students at this level to think about the answers to these questions and offer short verbal responses.

1. Look at page 295. How many years did Spain control parts of Latin America? (300)
2. Look at page 297. Why were the Indians and enslaved Africans ready for a change of government? (They worked hard but remained poor.)
3. Look at page 301. What cultures make up the Latin American culture? (Indian, Spanish, Portuguese, African, and French)
4. Look at the map on page 302. How many countries became independent in the nineteenth century? (eighteen)
5. Look at the timeline on page 303. When did the European colonization of Latin America take place? (from 1521 to 1800)

Intermediate Level Questions

Encourage students at this level to offer verbal responses or short written responses to the following questions.

1. Look at the section entitled Latin America Is Late to Industrialize. What happened to any effort to develop industry in the colonies? (It was crushed.)
2. Look at the section entitled Social Classes in the Colonies. How did the Spaniards feel about other groups in Latin America? (They felt superior to them.)
3. Look at the section entitled Dom Pedro. How was Brazil's revolution different from those in other countries? (There was no bloodshed.)
4. Look at the section entitled Governments of the New Nations. Why was there still no freedom after the nations became independent? (Dictators took over in most countries.)
5. Look at the section entitled Latin American Cultures. How are Spanish influences still seen in Latin America? (in language, religion, and architecture)

Advanced Level Questions

Encourage students at this level to provide written responses in complete sentences to the following questions.

1. Why did Spanish settlers make the Indians work for them? (Many Spanish settlers felt that they should not have to do certain kinds of work.)
2. Why did Spain and Portugal keep Latin American countries dependent? (Spain and Portugal kept Latin American countries dependent to exploit the resources and the people.)
3. What are characteristics of the Native American culture in Latin America? (They lived much like their ancestors, wore woven shawls, traveled to market along mountain roads on burros or llamas, played music on handmade instruments, and spun and weaved.)
4. What did all of the Latin American revolutionaries have in common? (Answers will vary. Accept all reasonable answers.)
5. What are some of the characteristics of Latin American culture? (Some of the characteristics of Latin American culture are the Spanish language, the Roman Catholic religion, the Spanish architecture, and the African influence in music.)

Closing the Chapter

Ask students to rewrite each heading in the chapter in the form of a question. For example, the section entitled Colonization could be rewritten as What did colonization mean for Latin America? and the section entitled Latin America Is Late to Industrialize could be rewritten as Why was Latin America late to industrialize? Once students have rewritten each heading in the form of a question, have students write answers for each of the questions.

ESL/ELL

Chapter 21: The United States Gains Power

pages 306–317

▶ Introducing the Chapter

Tapping Prior Knowledge

Ask students to preview the chapter by reading the headings and subheadings and by looking at the art and photos (on pages 306, 310, and 314 of the Student Edition), the map (on page 308 of the Student Edition), and the timeline (on page 315 of the Student Edition). Then, distribute the KWL chart on page 79 of this guide and ask students to complete the **K** and the **W** columns of the chart by writing what they know about the United States gaining power in the **K** column and what they would like to know in the **W** column. Ask students, *What do you want to know about the United States gaining power?*

Preteaching Vocabulary

Personalizing Vocabulary Begin by asking students to preview the chapter for five unfamiliar words or phrases and to record them in their Word Logs. Once students have identified these words and phrases, ask them to use their dictionaries to define them.

Identifying Essential Vocabulary Go over the pronunciation and meaning of each word and phrase in the box below. Then, ask students to write a sentence using a word or phrase from the box below and a Word to Know from page 307 of the Student Edition.

Word or Phrase	Meaning
threatened	said that you would cause pain, worry, or trouble if someone did not do what you wanted them to (p.307)
streamed	moved in the same direction (p.308)
mission	building in a foreign country where religious groups teach Christianity (p.309)
spirit	courage, energy, and determination (p.309)
battle cry	a shout used in war to encourage your side and frighten the enemy (p.309)
lay in ruins	was badly damaged (p.311)
naval base	place where people in the Navy live and work (p. 313)

▶ Applying Content Knowledge

From the Chapter: You Decide (page 314)

Ask students to read You Decide on page 314 of the Student Edition. Have students decide whether they believe that the explosion of the *Maine* was an accident or not. Then, have students form small groups of both view points. Ask students who believe that it was an accident to give reasons why they believe that and vice versa. Ask students, *Did anyone change his or her mind as a result of your group's discussion? What caused you to change your mind?*

Note-taking

Ask students to read Further Expansion: Alaska and Hawaii on pages 313 and 314 of the Student Edition about the acquisition of Alaska and Hawaii. Then, remind students of the difference between a fact and an opinion. Explain that a fact is a piece of information that can be measured or proven with evidence, and an opinion is an idea that other people can agree or disagree with. Then, have students find five factual statements about the acquisition of Alaska and Hawaii in the text. Ask students to write five opinions about the acquisition of Alaska and Hawaii based on the information in the text. You might wish to provide the following example as a model: *Fact: In 1867 Secretary of State William Seward had persuaded the United States to buy Alaska. Opinion: William Seward's idea to purchase Alaska was foolish.*

Using Visuals

Ask students to read Civil War on page 311 of the Student Edition and The Spanish-American War on page 314 of the Student Edition. Then, distribute the Venn Diagram on page 74 of this guide. Ask students to label the sections **The Civil War**, **Both**, and **The Spanish-American War**. Then, have students compare and contrast the Civil War and the Spanish-American War by listing details in the appropriate sections of the diagram. Ask students to use their completed Venn diagrams to write a summary. Students may wish to use this model as a topic sentence: *The Civil War was similar to the Spanish-American War because...*

Unit 8 • World History

Assessing Content Knowledge

Ask students to respond to the following questions. You may wish to encourage students with higher language proficiency to help beginning level students understand the questions.

Beginning Level Questions

Encourage students at this level to think about the answers to these questions and offer short verbal responses.

1. Look at the map on page 308. What does the green area on the map show? (the Louisiana Territory)
2. Look at page 309. What was the Battle of the Alamo? (a famous battle in the Texas war of independence)
3. Look at page 310. What treaty ended the war with Mexico? (the Treaty of Guadalupe Hidalgo)
4. Look at page 313. What two places did the transcontinental railroad link? (the eastern and western parts of the country)
5. Look at the timeline on page 315. When did the United States get the Panama Canal? (in 1903)

Intermediate Level Questions

Encourage students at this level to offer verbal responses or short written responses to the following questions.

1. Look at the section entitled Imperialism and the Monroe Doctrine. What was the purpose of the Monroe Doctrine? (to keep European countries out of the Americas)
2. Look at the section entitled A Growing United States: The Louisiana Purchase. What did the Louisiana Purchase accomplish? (It doubled the size of the United States.)
3. Look at the section entitled "Remember the Alamo!" Why was the Alamo important in the battle for Texas independence? (It was a place where Texans died in the war, but it also inspired Texans to fight.)
4. Look at the section entitled War with Mexico. What did the Treaty of Guadalupe Hidalgo give the United States? (It made the Rio Grande the boundary between Mexico and Texas, and in return for $15 million, it gave the United States more territory in the west.)
5. Look at the section entitled U.S. Power. What did the United States do in order to build the Panama Canal? (encouraged Panama to rebel against Colombia)

Advanced Level Questions

Encourage students at this level to provide written responses in complete sentences to the following questions.

1. How did Texas join the United States? (The Mexican general Santa Anna signed a peace treaty, and Texas became an independent nation, which then joined the United States.)
2. What was the main reason for the Civil War? (Abraham Lincoln could not allow the South to break up the Union and felt he had no choice but to go to war to save the Union.)
3. How did the United States acquire Hawaii? (Americans in Hawaii encouraged and led a revolt against the queen, and, in 1900, Hawaii became a territory of the United States.)
4. What were the causes of the Spanish-American War? (The United States wanted Spain out of the Caribbean; Americans sympathized with Cubans, who wanted independence; the United States wanted more power; and the U.S. battleship *Maine* exploded in Havana Harbor.)
5. Why was the Panama Canal important? (It became easier and faster for ships to travel between the Atlantic and Pacific, and it helped the United States to become stronger.)

Closing the Chapter

Ask students to complete the L column of the KWL charts that they began for the Tapping Prior Knowledge activity on page 42 of this guide. Then, have them use their completed KWL charts to write a summary about what they learned.

ESL/ELL

Chapter 22: Imperialism and the Far East

pages 318–331

Introducing the Chapter

Tapping Prior Knowledge
Ask students to preview the chapter by reading the headings and subheadings and by looking at the art (on pages 318, 320, and 327 of the Student Edition), the map (on page 321 of the Student Edition), and the timelines (on pages 325 and 329 of the Student Edition). Then, ask students to recall what they learned about imperialism in earlier chapters. Have students focus on the map of China on page 321 of the Student Edition. Ask students, *What natural borders can students see on the map that would help the country to remain isolated? What countries border China? What countries are near China? How big is China compared to other countries of the world?* Ask students, *How might imperialism affect a country as big as China?*

Preteaching Vocabulary

Personalizing Vocabulary Begin by asking students to preview the chapter for five unfamiliar words or phrases and to record them in their Word Logs. Once students have identified these words and phrases, ask them to use their dictionaries to define them.

Identifying Essential Vocabulary Go over the pronunciation and meaning of each word and phrase in the box below. Then, distribute an index card to each student. Ask each student to write a question on the index card using one or more of the vocabulary words or phrases. Then, have students select a partner to exchange cards with and have each student answer their partner's question.

Word or Phrase	Meaning
overthrew	got rid of by force (p.319)
looked down on	think that you are better than others (p.320)
seized	take away illegal goods (p.322)
be tried	to put someone on trial (p.322)
stern	very serious and strict (p.327)
stake claims	to say that you have a right to own something (p.329)

Applying Content Knowledge

From the Chapter: Learn More About It (page 324)
Ask students to read Learn More About It: The Boxer Rebellion on page 324 of the Student Edition. Distribute the Sequence of Events chart on page 77 of this guide. Ask students to organize the events that led up to and that followed the Boxer Rebellion.

Organizing Information
Distribute the Outline on page 76 of this guide. Write the following headings on the board and ask students to copy them onto their outlines. As students read the chapter, ask them to complete the outline with key details from the chapter.

> Topic: Imperialism and the Far East
> I. China
>   A. Dynasties
>   1. The Manchus Establish the Qing Dynasty
>   2. Sun Yatsen and the Chinese Nationalists
>   B. The Opium War
>   C. Chinese Rebellion
>   D. War With Japan
> II. Japan
>   A. Japan Opens Its Doors
>   B. A Modern Japan
>   C. Japanese Imperialism

Summarizing
Ask students to read The Manchus Establish the Qing Dynasty in China on pages 319–321 of the Student Edition and Sun Yatsen and the Chinese Nationalists on pages 325–326 of the Student Edition. Then, distribute the Venn Diagram on page 74 of this guide. Ask students to label the sections **The Qing Dynasty, Both,** and **Sun Yatsen and the Chinese Nationalists.** Then, have students compare and contrast the Qing Dynasty and Sun Yatsen and the Chinese Nationalists by listing details in the appropriate sections of the diagram. Ask students to use their completed Venn diagrams to write a summary. Students may wish to use this model as a topic sentence: *The Qing Dynasty was different from Sun Yatsen and the Chinese Nationalists because...*

44 Unit 8 • World History

Assessing Content Knowledge

Ask students to respond to the following questions. You may wish to encourage students with higher language proficiency to help beginning level students understand the questions.

Beginning Level Questions

Encourage students at this level to think about the answers to these questions and offer short verbal responses.

1. Look at page 319. What were two laws the Manchus passed against the Chinese? (A Manchu could not marry a Chinese person, and the laws forced Chinese men to wear a queue.)
2. Look at the map on page 321. What Chinese city is the Manchu Homeland close to? (Beijing)
3. Look at page 323. Why did China and Japan fight? (They both wanted Korea.)
4. Look at pages 325–326. Who was Sun Yatsen? (a Chinese doctor who led the revolution and overthrew the Manchu empire)
5. Look at the timeline on page 329. For how many years was Japan an isolated nation? (254)

Intermediate Level Questions

Encourage students at this level to offer verbal responses or short written responses to the following questions.

1. Look at the section entitled The Manchus Establish the Qing Dynasty in China. Why did the Manchus limit trade in China? (The Manchus looked down on the rest of the world.)
2. Look at the section entitled Chinese Rebellion. Which countries interfered in the Taiping Rebellion? (Great Britain, the United States, and other Western nations)
3. Look at the section entitled Japan Opens Its Doors. Why did the United States send Commodore Perry to Japan? (to deliver a letter from the President asking Japan to change its policies)
4. Look at the section entitled A Modern Japan. What were the two different opinions about the West in Japan? (Some wanted to drive the foreigners out of Japan; others wanted to accept the West and learn from it.)
5. Look at the section entitled Japanese Imperialism. What was Japanese imperialism? (Japan decided to set up overseas colonies to supply them with raw materials.)

Advanced Level Questions

Encourage students at this level to provide written responses in complete sentences to the following questions.

1. What were the terms of the Unequal Treaties? (China paid for the lost opium and the cost of the war; it opened ports to British trade; it gave the island of Hong Kong to Great Britain; and British citizens couldn't be tried for any crime in a Chinese court.)
2. How did isolationist policies hurt China? (China fell behind the Europeans in science and invention during those years.)
3. Why did Western countries interfere in the Taiping Rebellion? (They were afraid of losing their trade rights with China if the Manchus were overthrown.)
4. What were the results of the Chinese-Japanese War? (China had to give up much of its claim on Korea, and it had to give the island of Taiwan to the Japanese.)
5. Why was the Russo-Japanese War important for Japan? (For the first time, an Asian nation proved to be stronger than a European nation.)

Closing the Chapter

Ask students to use the outline they completed for the Organizing Information activity on page 44 of this guide to summarize what they learned.

ESL/ELL

Chapter 23: Imperialism and India

pages 332–343

Introducing the Chapter

Tapping Prior Knowledge
Ask students to preview the chapter by reading the headings and subheadings and by looking at the art and photos (on pages 332, 336, and 339 of the Student Edition), the map (on page 340 of the Student Edition), and the timeline (on page 341 of the Student Edition). Then, ask students, *How can the determination of one man change a nation?* Have students think about individuals who have done a great deal to improve the world. Encourage students to share their knowledge or experience of such a person and what this remarkable person has accomplished. Ask students, *What do people who have made a tremendous change to improve the lives of others mean to the world?*

Preteaching Vocabulary

Personalizing Vocabulary Begin by asking students to preview the chapter for five unfamiliar words or phrases and to record them in their Word Logs. Once students have identified these words and phrases, ask them to use their dictionaries to define them.

Identifying Essential Vocabulary Go over the pronunciation and meaning of each word in the box below. Then, ask students to create their own sentences for the words in the box below. Ask students to rewrite their sentences, leaving a blank space for the word. Have students exchange sentences and fill in the blanks of the other student's sentences.

Word	Meaning
landholders	people who own land (p.335)
officially	something that is public and formal (p.335)
backfired	had the opposite result from the one you intended (p.337)
founded	started (p.337)
linen	cloth made from the flax plant (p.339)
mourned	felt very sad because someone has died (p.341)

Applying Content Knowledge

From the Chapter: Learn More About It (page 335)
Ask students to read Learn More About It: The Sepoy Rebellion on page 335 of the Student Edition. Then, distribute the Venn diagram on page 74 of this guide. Ask students to label the sections **The Sepoys**, **Both**, and **The British**. Then, have students compare and contrast the Sepoys and the British. Ask students to use their completed Venn diagrams to write a summary about the differences between the Sepoys and the British using this topic sentence: *The Sepoys were different from the British because...*

Using Visuals
Ask students to study the map of India and Pakistan on page 340 of the Student Edition. Then, distribute the four-column chart on page 80 of this guide. Ask students to label the columns **Bodies of Water**, **Cities, Countries Bordering Pakistan**, and **Countries Bordering India**. Then, have students fill in the chart using the information in the map.

Using Resources
Ask students to read the section entitled Mahatma Gandhi on page 338 of the Student Edition. Then, distribute the Who, What, Why, Where, When, and How chart on page 72 of this guide. Have students write **Who was Mahatma Gandhi?** under **Who** in the chart; **What did Mahatma Gandhi do?** under **What** in the chart; **Why was Mahatma Gandhi important?** under **Why** in the chart; **Where did Mahatma Gandhi do what he did?** under **Where** in the chart; **When did Mahatma Gandhi do what he did?** under **When** in the chart; and **How did Mahatma Gandhi's actions affect the lives of others?** under **How** in the chart. Then, have students use their charts to write a summary.

Personalizing the Lesson
Ask students, *What are the advantages of nonviolent protests as a way to accomplish change?* Then, have students write a paragraph about an environmental or social issue that they think could be changed by using nonviolent protests.

Assessing Content Knowledge

Ask students to respond to the following questions. You may wish to encourage students with higher language proficiency to help beginning level students understand the questions.

Beginning Level Questions

Encourage students at this level to think about the answers to these questions and offer short verbal responses.

1. Look at page 334. How did ship captains of the East India Company become wealthy? (The company allowed them to use part of the cargo space to keep goods for themselves.)
2. Look at page 337. What was the Indian National Congress? (a group made up of educated Indians who wanted a revolution)
3. Look at page 338. What was the Amritsar Massacre? (British troops fired on an unarmed crowd and killed nearly 400 Indians.)
4. Look at page 341. How did Gandhi make the Hindu and Muslim leaders stop fighting in India? (He went on a fast and almost starved to death.)
5. Look at the timeline on page 341. How long was India a colony of Great Britain? (89 years)

Intermediate Level Questions

Encourage students at this level to offer verbal responses or short written responses to the following questions.

1. Look at the section entitled The British East India Company. What was the purpose of the war between France and Great Britain in India? (to control India)
2. Look at the section entitled The East India Company Rules. How did the British try to change India socially? (They imposed their own ways.)
3. Look at the section entitled British Rule. How did the British government try to improve life for the people of India? (It tried to solve poverty; helped farmers; set up hospitals; built railroads, factories, roads, and schools; and tried to do away with the caste system.)
4. Look at the section entitled Mahatma Gandhi. How did he resist the British? (through civil disobedience and nonviolent protests)
5. Look at the section entitled Gandhi Fasts for Peace. Why did the British offer independence to India? (They knew they would be forced to leave.)

Advanced Level Questions

Encourage students at this level to provide written responses in complete sentences to the following questions.

1. In the 1700s, what usually happened to a country that was weak? (Answers will vary. Possible answers might include colonization, being taken advantage of, civil war, and losing land it had claimed.)
2. How did the East India Company control India? (It began by taking sides in Indian civil wars and supporting Indian rulers who gave it favorable trade rights.)
3. What was the significance of the Sepoy Rebellion? (The Sepoy Rebellion convinced the government that the British East India Company couldn't be trusted with control of India.)
4. What was the purpose of the Indian National Congress? (The purpose was to plan a revolution.)
5. What events mark the beginning and the end of control of India by the East India Trading Company? (Clive's War marked the beginning, and the Sepoy Rebellion marked the end.)

Closing the Chapter

Distribute the Outline on page 76 of this guide. Write the following headings on the chalkboard and ask students to copy them onto their outlines. Ask students to complete their outlines with details from the chapter. Then, ask students to use their completed outlines to write a summary about what they learned.

Topic: Imperialism and India
  I. British East India Company
     A.
     B.
     C.
  II. British Rule
     A.
     B.
     C.
  III. Independence
     A.
     B.
     C.
  IV. Mahatma Gandhi
     A.
     B.
     C.

ESL/ELL

Chapter 24: Imperialism and Africa

pages 344–357

Introducing the Chapter

Tapping Prior Knowledge
Ask students to preview the chapter by reading the headings and subheadings and by looking at the photo (on page 344 of the Student Edition), the maps (on pages 346 and 349 of the Student Edition), the diagram (on page 353 of the Student Edition), and the timelines (on pages 347 and 355 of the Student Edition). Then, distribute the KWL chart on page 79 of this guide and ask students to use the map on page 346 of the Student Edition to complete the **K** and the **W** columns. Ask students, *What does this map tell you about the early civilizations of Africa?*

Preteaching Vocabulary
Personalizing Vocabulary Begin by asking students to preview the chapter for five unfamiliar words or phrases and to record them in their Word Logs. Once students have identified these words and phrases, ask them to use their dictionaries to define them.

Identifying Essential Vocabulary Go over the pronunciation and meaning of each word and phrase in the box below. Then, distribute the four-column chart on page 80 of this guide. Ask students to label the first column **Past Tense**, the second column **Present Tense**, the third column **Future Tense**, and the fourth column **Infinitive**. Then, have students complete the chart using the words and phrases in the box. For example, *arose* is the past tense of the verb and would be written under **Past Tense** in Row 1. The rest of the row would look like this: *arise, will arise, to arise*.

Word or Phrase	Meaning
arose	something that happened (p.345)
drive out	force someone or something to leave an area (p.346)
grew up	started to exist and then became bigger or more important (p.348)
dotted	spread things over a wide area (p.350)
abolished	officially ended a law or system (p.352)
drew up	prepared a written document (p.355)

Applying Content Knowledge

From the Chapter: History Fact (page 350)
Ask students to read the History Fact on page 350 of the Student Edition. Then, ask volunteers to tell the rest of the class what languages they speak or are spoken in their homes. Explain to students that English uses many words and phrases from other languages in the same way that Swahili uses many Arabic words. Tell students that phrases like *à la carte* and *prix fixe* are French phrases that have been borrowed and are used in the food industry. Ask students to suggest other words and phrases from other languages that the English language uses. These might include *hors d'oeuvres* (French—meal openers or appetizers), *sauté* (French—to fry), *à la mode* (French—on the top), and *salsa* (Spanish—sauce). Ask students to look at the languages they or their families speak as a starting point.

Using Visuals
Distribute the Timeline on page 75 of this guide. Ask students to review the timeline on page 347 of the Student Edition. Then, have students look back at timelines of Northern African and Mediterranean civilizations on pages 48, 56, 62, and 65 of the Student Edition. Ask students to work in small groups to make one timeline that incorporates the other five.

Organizing Information
Distribute the Outline on page 76 of this guide. Write the following headings on the chalkboard and ask students to copy them onto their outlines. As students read the chapter, ask them to complete the outline with key details from the chapter.

> **Topic: African Kingdoms**
> I. Kingdom of Ghana
> II. Kingdom of Mali
> III. Kingdom of Songhai
> IV. Other African Kingdoms

Assessing Content Knowledge

Ask students to respond to the following questions. You may wish to encourage students with higher language proficiency to help beginning level students understand the questions.

Beginning Level Questions

Encourage students at this level to think about the answers to these questions and offer short verbal responses.

1. Look at page 345. What were four civilizations of Africa? (Egyptian, Phoenicians, Romans, Arab conquerors)
2. Look at the map on page 346. Which African kingdoms are shown? (Egypt, Sudan, Kush, Aksum, Zimbabwe, Zulu, Cameroon, Songhai, Mali, Morocco, and Ghana)
3. Look at the timeline on page 347. Which civilization was ruled by Egypt in 1200 B.C.? (the Kush civilization)
4. Look at pages 348–349. What did Mansa Musa do that made him famous? (He made a pilgrimage to Mecca and gave out gold and other gifts along the way.)
5. Look at the timeline on page 355. What kingdom lasted the longest? (the kingdom of Ghana)

Intermediate Level Questions

Encourage students at this level to offer verbal responses or short written responses to the following questions.

1. Look at the section entitled Early Kingdoms. What goods did the caravans trade in western Africa? (tools, clothing, and salt)
2. Look at the section entitled Mansa Musa, the Mali King. How did Mali become a wealthy kingdom? (Mansa Musa encouraged caravan trade and then taxed it.)
3. Look at the section entitled The Europeans in Africa. What kept many European traders from traveling south across Africa by land? (the Sahara)
4. Look at the section entitled Europe Divides Up Africa. What was the purpose of the conference held in 1884 by European nations? (to set up rules for forming colonies in Africa)
5. Look at the section entitled Life in Colonial Africa. What improvements did Europeans make in Africa? (Railway systems, roads, and schools were built.)

Advanced Level Questions

Encourage students at this level to provide written responses in complete sentences to the following questions.

1. What caused conflict in the Kingdom of Ghana? (Ghana's rulers became Muslims, but most of the people in Ghana did not want to convert.)
2. How did Mohammed al-Mansur affect the kingdom of Songhai? (He attacked and defeated the Songhai.)
3. What two things led Europeans into Africa? (Imperialism and racism led Europeans into Africa.)
4. What was the purpose of the European missionaries in Africa? (European missionaries helped set up colonies with the intention of converting the Africans to Christianity.)
5. How did Europeans have a negative effect on the African culture? (They forced Africans to learn new ways; tried to make Africans feel inferior; forced Africans to accept European government, religion, and languages; and created boundaries without any thought of the tribes.)

Closing the Chapter

Ask students to complete the L column of the KWL charts that they began for the Tapping Prior Knowledge activity on page 48 of this guide. Then, have students use their completed KWL charts to write a summary about what they learned.

ESL/ELL

Chapter 25: The Unifications of Italy and Germany

pages 360–373

Introducing the Chapter

Tapping Prior Knowledge

Ask students to preview the chapter by reading the headings and subheadings and by looking at the art and photos (on pages 360, 365, 369, 370, and 371 of the Student Edition), the maps (on pages 362, 363, and 368 of the Student Edition), and the timeline (on page 371 of the Student Edition). Then, ask students what the word *nationalism* means. Encourage students to use their bilingual dictionaries to define the word. Have students suggest possible meanings of the word and work with students to arrive at a clear definition. Then, ask students, *What does it mean for a person to be nationalistic? For a country?*

Preteaching Vocabulary

Personalizing Vocabulary Begin by asking students to preview the chapter for five unfamiliar words or phrases and to record them in their Word Logs. Once students have identified these words and phrases, ask them to use their dictionaries to define them.

Identifying Essential Vocabulary Go over the pronunciation and meaning of each word and phrase in the box below. Then, ask students to combine one of these words or phrases with a vocabulary word from the list of Words to Know on page 361 of the Student Edition to create a sentence. Write the following sentence on the chalkboard for students to model: *The thief was <u>exiled</u> from <u>society</u>.*

Word or Phrase	Meaning
boundary	where one area of land ends and another begins (p.364)
barriers	problems that keep people from doing what they want (p.364)
exile	force to live away from home in a foreign land (p.365)
a firm hand	much control (p.369)
provinces	parts of a country with their own governments (p.370)

Applying Content Knowledge

From the Chapter: Words From the Past (page 369)

Ask students to read Words From the Past: Bismarck's Policy of "Blood and Iron" on page 369 of the Student Edition. Ask students, *Was Bismarck right? Can great questions be settled not by votes but by war?* Have students decide whether or not they believe that Bismarck was right. Then, have students form small groups to represent both viewpoints. Ask students who believe that he was right to give reasons why they believe that and vice versa. Ask students, *Did anyone change his or her mind as a result of your group's discussion? What caused you to change your mind?*

Organizing Information

Distribute the Outline on page 76 of this guide. As students read the chapter, ask them to use the outline to fill in the headings and corresponding details.

Summarizing

Distribute the Venn Diagram on page 74 of this guide. Ask students to label the sections **Nationalism in Italy**, **Both**, and **Nationalism in Germany.** Then, have students compare and contrast **Nationalism in Italy** and **Nationalism in Germany** by listing details in the appropriate sections of the diagram. Ask students to use their completed Venn diagrams to write a summary. Students may wish to use the following model topic sentences: *Nationalism in Italy was similar to nationalism in Germany because...* and *Nationalism in Italy was different from nationalism in Germany because...*

Note-taking

Ask students to read Nationalism in Italy on pages 362–364 of the Student Edition. Distribute the Sequence of Events chart on page 77 of this guide. Ask students to organize the events that led up to nationalism in Italy.

Assessing Content Knowledge

Ask students to respond to the following questions. You may wish to encourage students with higher language proficiency to help beginning level students understand the questions.

Beginning Level Questions

Encourage students at this level to think about the answers to these questions and offer short verbal responses.

1. Read page 361. What does nationalism lead people to do? (to honor their flag and to sing a national anthem)
2. Look at the map on page 362. How many kingdoms were in present-day Italy before unification? (15)
3. Look at page 364. What were the secret societies? (revolutionary groups of people who wanted to join together as one nation)
4. Look at page 370. Who did Prussia fight a war against in 1864? (Denmark)
5. Look at the timeline on page 371. How many years passed between the Italian Revolution and the unification of Italy? (22 years)

Intermediate Level Questions

Encourage students at this level to offer verbal responses or short written responses to the following questions.

1. Look at the section entitled Nationalism in Italy. Why was Napoleon important to nationalism in Italy? (Napoleon removed old boundaries and joined together the small kingdoms.)
2. Look at the section entitled Secret Societies. Why did Austria and the pope crush any ideas of unity? (They did not want their power threatened.)
3. Look at the section entitled The Soul. How was Sardinia affected by the revolution in 1848? (Sardinia was defeated.)
4. Look at the section entitled Nationalism in Germany. Why didn't Austria want German unity? (Austrians thought they could remain more powerful with German states divided.)
5. Look at the section entitled The German Nation. What were the two main features of the new Germany? (It was not democratic, and it had a strong tradition of militarism.)

Advanced Level Questions

Encourage students at this level to provide written responses in complete sentences to the following questions.

1. Why were the three revolutionaries called The Soul, The Brain, and The Sword? (Answers will vary. Possible answers might suggest that these names reflected the role that each man played.)
2. How did Prussia indirectly help Rome become part of Italy? (France was fighting a war against Prussia and took its troops out of Rome to help fight the Prussians. The pope's own small army alone could not fight off the Italian troops.)
3. What did Bismarck decide was the best way to join the states under one rule? (He decided that he would rally them together against one common enemy.)
4. How did Germans develop their strong military? (They took pride in a strong military, gave their soldiers respect and honor, made it a privilege and an honor to fight for the empire, and geared business toward the support of the army.)
5. What would you have thought Germany's undemocratic government and strong tradition of militarism would have meant for the future of Germany? (Answers will vary. Possible answers might include war, early successes, and eventual defeat.)

Closing the Chapter

Ask students to rewrite each of the Learning Objectives listed on page 360 of the Student Edition in the form of a question. For example, the first one could be rewritten as What is nationalism? Why did it develop? Once students have rewritten each Learning Objective in the form of a question, have students write answers for each of the questions. Then, ask students to use their answers to write a summary about what they learned.

ESL/ELL

World War I
pages 374–387

▶ Introducing the Chapter

Tapping Prior Knowledge
Ask students to preview the chapter by reading the headings and subheadings and by looking at the art and photos (on pages 374, 378, and 380 of the Student Edition), the maps (on pages 376 and 383 of the Student Edition), the chart (on page 384 of the Student Edition), and the timeline (on page 385 of the Student Edition). Then, ask students to brainstorm a list of things that they already know about World War I. Write these items on the chalkboard. Then, ask students, *Why is it important to know the reasons why a war took place?*

Preteaching Vocabulary
Personalizing Vocabulary Begin by asking students to preview the chapter for five unfamiliar words or phrases and to record them in their Word Logs. Once students have identified these words and phrases, ask them to use their dictionaries to define them.

Identifying Essential Vocabulary Go over the pronunciation and meaning of each word and phrase in the box below. Then, distribute the four-column chart on page 80 of this guide. Have students create a chart using the following headings: **Word or Phrase, Meaning Clues From the Text, Definition,** and **My Sentence.**

Word or Phrase	Meaning
strained	unfriendly, not trusting (p.375)
tension	a feeling that exists when people or countries do not trust each other (p.376)
bitter enemies	groups or individuals who hate each other (p.376)
shots rang out	the sound of a gun being fired (p.377)
given up	stop trying to do something (p.382)
a blow	something that makes you feel unhappy, sad, or disappointed, or that damages your confidence or pride (p.382)
in vain	without success (p.385)

▶ Applying Content Knowledge

From the Chapter: Learn More About It (page 381)
Ask students to read Learn More About It: Wartime Inventions on page 381 of the Student Edition. Then, distribute the Spider Web on page 73 of this guide. Ask students to write **Wartime Inventions** in the center circle and list on the spokes of the web the four inventions that were perfected to meet war needs. Then, have students list specific details about each of the wartime inventions. Ask students, *Why are new inventions perfected quickly during wartime?*

Using Visuals
Ask students to compare the maps on pages 376 and 383 of the Student Edition. Distribute the Venn diagram on page 74 of this guide. Ask students to label the sections **Europe In 1914, Both,** and **Europe After World War I.** Then, have students compare and contrast Europe in 1914 and Europe after World War I by listing details in the appropriate sections of the diagram. Ask students to use their completed Venn diagrams to write a summary. Students may wish to use the following model topic sentence: *After World War I, Europe changed because…* Suggest that students' answers address the changes that countries like Russia, Austria-Hungary, and Germany went through after the war.

Role-playing
Ask students to take the point of view of one of the countries that participated in the war and role-play a leader of that country explaining the political reasons why they wanted to declare war.

Organizing Information
Distribute the Outline on page 76 of this guide. Write the following headings on the chalkboard and ask students to copy them onto their outlines. As students read the chapter, ask them to use the outline to fill in the corresponding details.

> Topic: World War I
>   I. Before the War
> II. During the War
> III. The End of the War

Assessing Content Knowledge

Ask students to respond to the following questions. You may wish to encourage students with higher language proficiency to help beginning level students understand the questions.

Beginning Level Questions

Encourage students at this level to think about the answers to these questions and offer short verbal responses.

1. Look at page 375. What are two reasons nations wanted a strong military? (nationalism and imperialism)
2. Look at the map on page 376. Which countries belonged to the Allied Powers and which countries belonged to the Central Powers? (See page 376.)
3. Look at page 377. What incident began World War I? (the assassination of Archduke Ferdinand and his wife by a Serbian revolutionary)
4. Look at page 379. Who was the President of the United States during World War I? (President Woodrow Wilson)
5. Look at page 382. What was the Treaty of Versailles? (the peace treaty that was signed after WWI)

Intermediate Level Questions

Encourage students at this level to offer verbal responses or short written responses to the following questions.

1. Look at the section entitled The Balance of Power. Why did the nations of Europe form alliances? (to help and protect each other in case of war)
2. Look at the section entitled Trench Warfare. How did soldiers fight this war? (Many fought in a network of trenches on one of the three fronts.)
3. Look at the section entitled The United States Enters the War. What caused Russia to pull out of the war? (the Russian Revolution)
4. Look at the section entitled The Treaty of Versailles. What were the terms of the Treaty of Versailles? (Germany lost its colonies and Alsace and Lorraine; it took the blame for the war; it paid many of the costs from the war; and it promised to disarm. The Ottoman Empire ended, and Britain controlled Arab lands that had been ruled by the Turks.)
5. Look at the section entitled The League of Nations: A Peacekeeper. Why was the League of Nations created? (Leaders of the world's nations decided that there must be a better way to solve conflicts between nations.)

Advanced Level Questions

Encourage students at this level to provide written responses in complete sentences to the following questions.

1. How did imperialism contribute to military build-ups? (Imperialism meant that nations had colonies that they wanted to keep under their control.)
2. Do you think that the United States would have entered the war if the *Lusitania* had not been torpedoed? (Answers will vary. Accept all reasonable responses.)
3. Why are many inventions created or improved during wartime? (Answers will vary. Possible answers might include that the need for a particular invention can be especially urgent during wartime.)
4. Look at the chart on page 384. Why do you think the United States had fewer casualties than the other Allies? (The United States entered the war late; the war was not fought in the Americas.)
5. Why was it unlikely that the League of Nations could be a successful peacekeeper? (Not all nations joined the League of Nations, and it had no army to enforce its decisions.)

Closing the Chapter

Ask students to use the outline they completed for the Organizing Information activity on page 52 of this guide to summarize what they learned.

ESL/ELL

Chapter 27: Revolution in Russia: The Birth of the Soviet Union
pages 388–405

▶ Introducing the Chapter

Tapping Prior Knowledge
Ask students to preview the chapter by reading the headings and subheadings and by looking at the art and photos (on pages 388, 390, 391, 392, 394, 396, 400, and 401 of the Student Edition), the map (on page 399 of the Student Edition), and the timeline (on page 403 of the Student Edition). Then, direct students to the title of the chapter, Revolution in Russia: The Birth of the Soviet Union. Encourage students to recall the times when they have seen the word *revolution* in earlier chapters. Then, remind students that history is a collection of stories. Ask students, *Based on the title of the chapter, what do you think this story will be about? How can revolution lead to the birth of a new nation?*

Preteaching Vocabulary
Personalizing Vocabulary Begin by asking students to preview the chapter for five unfamiliar words or phrases and to record them in their Word Logs. Once students have identified these words and phrases, ask them to use their dictionaries to define them.

Identifying Essential Vocabulary Go over the pronunciation and meaning of each word and phrase in the box below. Then, ask students to classify each of the following words and phrases as a noun (n.), an adjective (adj.), or and adverb (adv.).

Word or Phrase	Meaning
wastelands (n.)	land that is empty, ugly, and not used for anything (p.389)
varied (adj.)	different (p.389)
dreadfully (adv.)	extremely; very (p.391)
scarcely (adv.)	almost not at all; just barely (p.395)
classless society (n.)	a society in which people were not divided into different social classes (p.397)
resistance (n.)	the act of fighting against someone or something who is attacking or controlling you (p.398)
hard to come by (adj.)	hard to get (p.402)

▶ Applying Content Knowledge

From the Chapter: Words From the Past (page 396)
Ask students to read Words From the Past: Karl Marx and the *Communist Manifesto* on page 396 of the Student Edition. Then, remind students that an opinion is an idea that other people can agree or disagree with. Then, have students write three opinions that Karl Marx expressed based on the information in the text. You might wish to provide the following example as a model. *Opinion: A spectre spirit is haunting Europe.* Once students finish listing the opinions, ask them to write *their* opinion of his beliefs (agree or disagree) and give one or two reasons that support their opinion.

Note-taking
Ask students to read pages 397–398 of the Student Edition. Have students take notes on the steps that led up to the Bolshevik Revolution. Then, distribute the Sequence of Events chart on page 77 of this guide and ask students to organize the steps that led up to the Bolshevik Revolution. Ask students to use their Sequence of Events charts to write a summary about the steps that led up to the Bolshevik Revolution.

Summarizing
Ask students to read Peter the Great: A "Window to the West" on pages 392–394 of the Student Edition. Then, distribute the Who, What, Why, Where, When, and How chart on page 72 of this guide. Have students write **Who was Peter the Great?** under **Who** in the chart; **What did Peter the Great want to do?** under **What** in the chart; **Why was Peter the Great important?** under **Why** in the chart; **Where did Peter the Great have a great influence?** under **Where** in the chart; **When did Peter the Great do what he wanted to do?** under **When** in the chart; and **How did Peter the Great's actions affect history?** under **How** in the chart. Have students complete their charts using the information from the text.

54 Unit 9 • World History

ESL/ELL

▶ Assessing Content Knowledge

Ask students to respond to the following questions. You may wish to encourage students with higher language proficiency to help beginning level students understand the questions.

Beginning Level Questions

Encourage students at this level to think about the answers to these questions and offer short verbal responses.

1. Look at page 389. What is the geography of Russia like? (thick forests, deserts, mountains, and long rivers)
2. Look at page 391. Who was the first czar of Russia? (Ivan IV, Ivan the Terrible)
3. Look at page 395. Why did the czar's soldiers kill or wound hundreds of people? (Workers wanted higher wages and a voice in government.)
4. Look at the map on page 399. What does *U.S.S.R.* stand for? (Union of Soviet Socialist Republics)
5. Look at the timeline on page 403. In what year did Catherine the Great become the ruler of Russia? (1762)

Intermediate Level Questions

Encourage students at this level to offer verbal responses or short written responses to the following questions.

1. Look at the section entitled The Early History of Russia. Who are the different groups that lived in what is now Russia? (Slavs, Vikings, and Mongols)
2. Look at the section entitled Peter the Great: A "Window to the West." What was the "Window to the West?" (a port on the Baltic Sea)
3. Look at the section entitled "Bloody Sunday" and the 1905 Revolution. What led to "Bloody Sunday?" (Peasants marched in St. Petersburg, demanding higher wages and a voice in government.)
4. Look at the section entitled World War I and the Overthrow of Czar Nicholas II. What were the effects of World War I on Russia? (It drained supplies, killed many men, and created food shortages.)
5. Look at the section entitled Lenin and the Bolshevik Revolution. Who were the Bolsheviks? (a revolutionary Communist group that overthrew the government)

Advanced Level Questions

Encourage students at this level to provide written responses in complete sentences to the following questions.

1. What did many of the Russian czars have in common? (Answers will vary. Accept all reasonable responses.)
2. How did Lenin differ from Karl Marx? (Marx had pictured a society that would someday have no need for government. Lenin's government was strict.)
3. How did Lenin fail to deliver what the Bolsheviks had promised? (The police made secret arrests; the government took businesses; farmers were ordered to turn their crops over to the government; and the clergy were arrested to eliminate religion.)
4. Why was the U.S.S.R said to be behind an Iron Curtain? (Soviet people were not free to travel outside the country, and the government controlled information from outside the country.)
5. How did Stalin control the U.S.S.R? (Answers will vary. Possible answers include fear, control of information, and harsh punishments for opposing him.)

▶ Closing the Chapter

Ask students to rewrite each of the Learning Objectives listed on page 388 of the Student Edition in the form of a question. For example, the first one could be rewritten as What were the main events in Russia's history? Once students have rewritten each Learning Objective in the form of a question, have students write answers for each of the questions. Then, ask students to use their answers to write a summary about what they learned.

ESL/ELL

Chapter 28: World War II
pages 406–427

▶ Introducing the Chapter

Tapping Prior Knowledge
Ask students to preview the chapter by reading the headings and subheadings and by looking at the art and photos (on pages 406, 408, 409, 412, 413, 417, 420, 422, and 424 of the Student Edition), the map (on page 414 of the Student Edition), and the timeline (on page 425 of the Student Edition). Then, ask students to tell what they know about World War II. Write students' suggestions on the chalkboard. Ask students, *Why is it important to know the causes of a war?* Students should suggest that knowing the causes of a war could keep history from repeating itself.

Preteaching Vocabulary
Personalizing Vocabulary Begin by asking students to preview the chapter for five unfamiliar words or phrases and to record them in their Word Logs. Once students have identified these words and phrases, ask them to use their dictionaries to define them.

Identifying Essential Vocabulary Go over the pronunciation and meaning of each word and phrase in the box below. Then, ask students to combine one of these words or phrases with a vocabulary word or phrase from the list of Words to Know on page 407 of the Student Edition to create a sentence. Write the following sentence on the chalkboard for students to model: <u>Fascists</u> insist on <u>absolute rule</u>.

Word or Phrase	Meaning
absolute rule	complete rule with no limits (p.408)
wounded pride	respect that has been damaged (p.409)
axis	an imaginary line that a large round object, like the Earth, spins around (p.409)
fiery speeches	speeches that show strong emotions, like anger and excitement (p.410)
mindless hatred	angry dislike for someone that is completely stupid and without purpose (p.410)
set forth	to begin a journey (p.410)

▶ Applying Content Knowledge

From the Chapter: Words From the Past (page 412)
Ask students to read Words From the Past: Winston Churchill, June 4, 1940, on page 412 of the Student Edition. Then, distribute the Spider Web on page 73 of this guide. Ask students to write **World War II Figures** in the center circle and **Churchill, Roosevelt, Hitler**, and **Mussolini** on the spokes of the web. Then, have students list specific details about each figure. Ask students, *What effect(s) did each of the leaders have during World War II?*

Using Visuals
Ask students to read the section entitled The Costs of War on page 423. Then, distribute pieces of graph paper. Have students create a bar graph to reflect the losses in World War II.

Organizing Information
Distribute the Sequence of Events chart on page 77 of this guide and ask students to organize the events in Hitler's rise to power and his plan to conquer Europe. Ask students to use their Sequence of Events charts to write a summary.

Note-taking
Distribute the Outline on page 76 of this guide. Write the following headings on the chalkboard and ask students to copy them onto their outlines. As students read the chapter, ask them to add headings and complete the outline with key details from the chapter.

> Topic: World War II
> I. Before the War
>   A. The Rise of the Dictators
>   B.
>   C.
> II. During the War
>   A. The Battle of Britain
>   B. Hitler Turns on the Soviet Union
>   C. The Holocaust
>   D. The United States Declares War
> III. The End of the War
>   A. The Costs of the War
>   B. The United Nations

ESL/ELL

▶ Assessing Content Knowledge

Ask students to respond to the following questions. You may wish to encourage students with higher language proficiency to help beginning level students understand the questions.

Beginning Level Questions

Encourage students at this level to think about the answers to these questions and offer short verbal responses.

1. Look at page 407. What happened during the Great Depression? (Businesses went broke; workers were out of jobs; farmers could not sell their crops; banks closed; and poverty spread throughout the world.)
2. Look at the map on page 414. What were the six major battles of the war? (the Normandy Invasion, the Battle of the Bulge, Berlin, Stalingrad, Tunis, and El Alamein)
3. Look at page 415. What happened to Hitler's army in the U.S.S.R.? (Nazi soldiers froze.)
4. Look at page 422. On what two cities were atomic bombs dropped? (Hiroshima and Nagasaki)
5. Look at the timeline of World War II on page 425. How many years passed between Hitler taking power and the beginning of World War II? (six years)

Intermediate Level Questions

Encourage students at this level to offer verbal responses or short written responses to the following questions.

1. Look at the section entitled The Rise of Dictators. What conditions led to the rise of dictators? (the hard conditions of the Great Depression)
2. Look at the section entitled Hitler. What did Hitler promise the German people? (He promised to return Germany to power and glory.)
3. Look at the section entitled Hitler's *Blitzkrieg*. Why was the *blitzkrieg* effective for Germany? (It made it possible for Germany to defeat Poland, Norway, Denmark, the Netherlands, Luxembourg, Belgium, and France.)
4. Look at the section entitled The Holocaust. What was the Holocaust? (Hitler's efforts to destroy anyone who did not fit his idea of the super race)
5. Look at the section entitled The United Nations. What is the purpose of the United Nations? (to protect world peace and to safeguard human rights)

Advanced Level Questions

Encourage students at this level to provide written responses in complete sentences to the following questions.

1. How did the British retaliate against Germany? (They fought back, worked out air-raid plans, and remained strong.)
2. Why was the United States' entry into World War II so important? (The Allies now had the military commitment of the United States.)
3. What were three major turning points of the war? (Answers may vary. Possible answers might include the German defeat in the Soviet Union; the entry of the United States into the war; the failure of the London Blitz; or the defeat of German and Italian forces in Africa.)
4. Why do you think Britain and France did not stop Hitler sooner? (Answers will vary. Possible answers might include their hopes that trying to satisfy him would stop him, their desire for peace, or their fear of war.)
5. Do you think the atomic bomb should have been used? Explain your answer. (Answers will vary. Accept all reasonable responses.)

▶ Closing the Chapter

Ask students to use the outline they completed for the Note-taking activity on page 56 of this guide to write a summary about what they learned.

ESL/ELL

Chapter 29 — Changes in Europe
pages 430–441

▶ Introducing the Chapter

Tapping Prior Knowledge
Ask students to preview the chapter by reading the headings and subheadings and by looking at the art and photos (on pages 430, 436, and 438) of the Student Edition, the map (on page 433 of the Student Edition), and the timeline (on page 439 of the Student Edition). Then, ask students to think about a time when they had a disagreement with someone. Ask students, *How did you feel once the disagreement was over? How did the disagreement affect the future of your relationship?* Then, ask students, *How might the world have been affected once World War II was over?*

Preteaching Vocabulary

Personalizing Vocabulary Begin by asking students to preview the chapter for five unfamiliar words or phrases and to record them in their Word Logs. Once students have identified these words and phrases, ask them to use their dictionaries to define them.

Identifying Essential Vocabulary Go over the pronunciation and meaning of each word and phrase in the box below. Then, distribute the four-column chart on page 80 of this guide. Ask students to label the columns **Word, Sentence From the Text, Synonym,** and **My Sentence.** Ask students to complete their charts by writing the word in the first column, the sentence in which the word is used in the second column, a synonym for the word in the third column, and a sentence of their own using the word in the fourth column. To find synonyms for each word, ask students to use their bilingual dictionaries and context clues from the Student Edition.

Word or Phrase	Meaning
war-torn	destroyed by war (p.431)
shambles	a place where there is a lot of damage, destruction, and confusion (p.432)
stakes	a situation where you may gain or lose a lot (p.436)
peaks	highest points or levels (p.438)

▶ Applying Content Knowledge

From the Chapter: Timeline Study (page 439)
Ask students to read Timeline Study on page 439 of the Student Edition. Ask students to suppose that a wall divided their city that was designed to keep them from ever leaving. Ask students, *How would you feel?* Encourage students to discuss their thoughts and feelings about such a wall. Then, ask students, *How do you suppose the East Berliners felt?*

Using Visuals
Ask students to study the timeline on page 439 of the Student Edition. Then, have students work with a partner to write a question and a corresponding answer for each item on the timeline. Then, have students partner with another pair to answer the other's questions.

Using Realia
Explain to students that the decades following the end of World War II led to many changes in the everyday lives of people in the United States. Ask students to work in groups and choose one of the decades—1950s, 1960s, 1970s, 1980s, or 1990s—to research for changes in clothing, cars, homes, popular entertainment, sports, and so on. Then, distribute the Venn diagram on page 74 of this guide. Ask students to label the sections **Life During World War II, Both,** and **Life in the ____.** Then, have students compare and contrast what life was like during World War II and what life was like in the decade they chose by listing details in the appropriate sections of the diagram. Ask students to use their completed Venn diagrams to write a summary. Students may wish to use the following model topic sentence: *Life in the ____ was different from life during World War II because...* You may wish to ask students to make a poster for their decade and illustrate it using magazine cutouts, Internet pictures, and newspaper clippings. You may also wish to ask each group to prepare a short oral report of the decade it chose, describing how it differed from life during World War II.

58 Unit 10 • World History

Assessing Content Knowledge

Ask students to respond to the following questions. You may wish to encourage students with higher language proficiency to help beginning level students understand the questions.

Beginning Level Questions

Encourage students at this level to think about the answers to these questions and offer short verbal responses.

1. Look at the map on page 433. What two seas are shown? (the North Sea and the Baltic Sea)
2. Look at page 435. Who did the Soviet Union create an alliance with in 1955? (its Communist allies in Eastern Europe)
3. Look at pages 436–437. Who was Nikita Khrushchev? (the Soviet premier after Stalin's death)
4. Look at page 439. What were the SALT talks? (Strategic Arms Limitations Talks)
5. Look at the timeline on page 439. In what year did the first SALT talks take place? (1972)

Intermediate Level Questions

Encourage students at this level to offer verbal responses or short written responses to the following questions.

1. Look at the section entitled Germany in Ruins. Why was Germany divided into East Germany and West Germany? (The Soviets would not agree to a unified Germany, so the Soviets controlled the east, and the United States, Great Britain, and France controlled the west.)
2. Look at the section entitled The Cold War. What was the Truman Doctrine? (a plan for military and economic support for any country fighting communism)
3. Look at the section entitled NATO. What was the purpose of the Warsaw Pact? (The Soviet Union created an alliance with its Communist allies in Eastern Europe to balance the NATO alliance.)
4. Look at the section entitled Economic Alliances. What was the economic alliance that developed in Europe? (the European Union)
5. Look at the section entitled Soviets and Americans Talk of Peace. Why did the United States and the Soviet Union talk of peace? (They both realized that another war would bring disaster.)

Advanced Level Questions

Encourage students at this level to provide written responses in complete sentences to the following questions.

1. Why do you think that the Soviet Union and its Communist satellites refused to accept the Marshall Plan? (Answers will vary. Possible answers include the idea that they wanted to remain Communist and did not want to be indebted to any democratic governments.)
2. What was the purpose of having Great Britain, France, the United States, and the Soviet Union control Germany? (The purpose was to keep order and help rebuild the German economy.)
3. How did the cold war occur? (The United States and the Soviet Union were the two superpowers, but they disagreed on what an ideal society should be like. The disputes and tensions that grew became known as the cold war.)
4. What kind of leader was Nikita Khrushchev? Explain your answer. (Answers will vary. Possible answers include that he was a good leader because he improved the lives of the people of the Soviet Union.)
5. Why were the SALT talks important? (They were important because both the United States and the Soviet Union agreed to set some limits on nuclear arms.)

Closing the Chapter

Ask students to summarize the most important points from the chapter by writing two facts for each subheading in the chapter. Then, have students use those facts to write a summary about what they have learned.

ESL/ELL

Chapter 30 — Changes in Asia and Africa
pages 442–463

Introducing the Chapter

Tapping Prior Knowledge
Ask students to preview the chapter by reading the headings and subheadings and by looking at the photos (on pages 442, 445, 447, 453, 454, 455, and 458 of the Student Edition), the map (on page 459 of the Student Edition), and the timeline (on page 461 of the Student Edition). Then, ask students to rewrite each of the Learning Objectives on page 442 of the Student Edition in the form of a question. For example, the first one could be rewritten as What were some of India's problems? Ask students, *What would you like to know about Asia? About Africa?*

Preteaching Vocabulary
Personalizing Vocabulary Begin by asking students to preview the chapter for five unfamiliar words or phrases and to record them in their Word Logs. Once students have identified these words and phrases, ask them to use their dictionaries to define them.

Identifying Essential Vocabulary Go over the pronunciation and meaning of each word in the box below. Then, ask students to classify each of the following words as a noun (n.) or a verb (v.).

Word	Meaning
shortages (n.)	situation in which there is not enough of something that people need (p.444)
clashed (v.)	fought or argued (p.444)
disputes (n.)	arguments over who owns or controls something (p.444)
expelled (v.)	to make someone leave (p.446)
truce (n.)	an agreement between enemies to stop fighting for a period of time (p.449)
turmoil (n.)	a situation in which there is confusion, excitement, and trouble (p.453)
famine (n.)	a situation in which a large number of people have little or no food for a long time, causing many people to die (p.457)
drought (n.)	a long period of dry weather when there is not enough water (p.457)

Applying Content Knowledge

From the Chapter: African Nations Become Independent (page 459)
Ask students to study the map entitled African Nations Become Independent on page 459 of the Student Edition. Distribute the Timeline on page 75 of this guide and ask students to complete the timeline according to the year each country became independent.

Organizing Information
Distribute the Idea Web on page 81 of this guide. Ask students to write **Problem-Solution** in the center shape and **India, China, Korea, Vietnam,** and **Japan** in the surrounding ovals. Then, ask students to complete their Idea Webs by listing two problems for each of these countries and two solutions that each of the countries has attempted.

Using Manipulatives
Distribute index cards. Ask students to work with a partner and use the timeline on page 461 of the Student Edition to write questions about the various countries. Ask students to write each question on the front of an index card and its answer on the back of the index card. Then, have each pair of students exchange their cards with another pair of students and have partners take turns asking each other the questions. You may wish to combine all of the cards, shuffle them, and then redistribute them to pairs of students.

Personalizing the Lesson
Ask students to work in small groups to choose a country in Africa or Asia that they think is interesting and have them do research to learn more about it. Then, ask students to create a poster for that country. Ask students to try to include information about as many of the following topics as possible: people, geography, culture (food, clothing, music, art), history, religion(s), economy, and political or social issues. You may wish to ask students to present their posters to the rest of the class along with a brief report explaining what their research uncovered.

60 Unit 10 • World History

Assessing Content Knowledge

Ask students to respond to the following questions. You may wish to encourage students with higher language proficiency to help beginning level students understand the questions.

Beginning Level Questions

Encourage students at this level to think about the answers to these questions and offer short verbal responses.

1. Look at page 443. What religious groups controlled India and Pakistan? (Muslims in Pakistan and Hindus in India)
2. Look at page 447. Who was Mao Zedong? (Communist leader of the People's Republic of China)
3. Look at page 455. What happened after the Khmer Rouge lost its power in Cambodia? (National elections were held.)
4. Look at the map on page 459. What country is farthest south? (South Africa)
5. Look at the timeline on page 461. How many years did the Korean War last? (three years)

Intermediate Level Questions

Encourage students at this level to offer verbal responses or short written responses to the following questions.

1. Look at the section entitled The Cultural Revolution. What was the purpose of the Cultural Revolution? (to build Communist loyalty)
2. Look at the section entitled The United States Gets Involved. What was the domino theory? (if one country became Communist, others would too.)
3. Look at the section entitled Americans Protest U.S. Involvement. What leaders were assassinated in the United States during the 1960s? (John F. Kennedy, Robert Kennedy, Malcolm X, and Martin Luther King, Jr.)
4. Look at the section entitled A Changing South Africa. What were the apartheid laws in South Africa? (Races were separated by where they could live, what property they could own, and what businesses they could run; there were curfews and separate facilities for black people.)
5. Look at the section entitled Africa Today. What are some of the problems African nations struggle to solve? (poverty, disease, food shortages and starvation, lack of education and hospitals, and civil wars)

Advanced Level Questions

Encourage students at this level to provide written responses in complete sentences to the following questions.

1. How is Japan affected by its geography? (It has little land to grow food and depends on imports. It is overcrowded, causing pollution and housing shortages.)
2. Why did the United States fight wars in Korea and Vietnam? (The United States fought wars in Korea and Vietnam to stop the spread of communism.)
3. What risks did refugees face when escaping by boat? (Answers will vary. Possible answers might include that the boat could fall apart or sink and that the refugees would drown; that the refugees could be attacked and killed by sharks; that the refugees could get lost or have to deal with harsh weather, winds, or storms at sea.)
4. What kinds of problems can freedom bring? (Some problems include poverty, disease, food shortages and starvation, lack of education, and civil wars.)
5. What helped to bring about the end of apartheid in South Africa? (Sanctions and other pressures from the United States and other countries and people of the world.)

Closing the Chapter

Ask students to answer the questions they wrote for the Tapping Prior Knowledge activity on page 60 of this guide. Have students use the answers to their questions to write a summary about what they learned.

ESL/ELL

Chapter 31: The Middle East
pages 464–481

▶ Introducing the Chapter

Tapping Prior Knowledge
Ask students to preview the chapter by reading the headings and subheadings and by looking at the photos (on pages 464, 469, 473, 474, 476, and 478 of the Student Edition), the maps (on pages 466 and 471 of the Student Edition), and the timeline (on page 479 of the Student Edition). Then, ask students what the words *tension* and *conflict* mean. Then, ask students, *What does it mean to be tense? What does it mean to have a conflict? How might tension and conflict affect peoples' lives?*

Preteaching Vocabulary
Personalizing Vocabulary Begin by asking students to preview the chapter for five unfamiliar words or phrases and to record them in their Word Logs. Once students have identified these words and phrases, ask them to use their dictionaries to define them.

Identifying Essential Vocabulary Go over the pronunciation and meaning of each word and phrase in the box below. Then, ask students to work in groups to write a paragraph using the words and phrases. Have each student in the group write one sentence using one of the words or phrases. Then, have the groups put their sentences together to create a paragraph. Ask each group to rewrite their paragraph, substituting blank lines for the vocabulary words and phrases. Have groups trade paragraphs and complete them by filling in the missing vocabulary words and phrases.

Word or Phrase	Meaning
meanwhile	while something else is happening (p.465)
homeland	land made by or for a particular group to live in (p.466)
refugees	people who have been forced to leave their country (p.468)
stalemated	be in a situation in which it seems impossible to settle an argument (p.472)
cease-fire	an agreement to stop fighting for a period of time (p.474)
heated conflict	intense disagreement (p.475)

▶ Applying Content Knowledge

From the Chapter: Learn More About It (page 470)
Ask students to read Learn More About It: Anwar Sadat on page 470 of the Student Edition. Then, ask students if they know what the Nobel Peace Prize is. Write students' suggestions on the chalkboard. Then, distribute the KWL chart on page 79 of this guide and ask students to complete the **K** and the **W** columns of the chart by writing what they know about the Nobel Peace Prize in the **K** column and what they would like to know about the Nobel Peace Prize in the **W** column. Then, have students do research at a library or on the Internet to find answers to the items in the **W** column of their charts. Tell students that they will complete the **L** column after they complete their research. Encourage students to share information from their research with the rest of the class. You may wish to have students write a paragraph that summarizes their charts. Ask students, *What kind of leader was Anwar Sadat to have been awarded the Nobel Peace Prize?*

Note-taking
Distribute the Sequence of Events chart on page 77 of this guide. Ask students to organize the events that led up to the Persian Gulf War.

Organizing Information
Distribute the Outline on page 76 of this guide. As students read the chapter, ask them to add headings and complete the outline with key details from the chapter.

> Topic: The Middle East
> I. Nationalism in the Middle East
>   A.
>   B.
> II. A Jewish Homeland in Palestine
>   A. The State of Israel
>   B. Refugees of War
> III. Conflicts in the Middle East
>   A.
>   B.
> IV. Life in the Middle East
>   A.
>   B.

Assessing Content Knowledge

Ask students to respond to the following questions. You may wish to encourage students with higher language proficiency to help beginning level students understand the questions.

Beginning Level Questions

Encourage students at this level to think about the answers to these questions and offer short verbal responses.

1. Look at the photo on page 464. Who are the men in the photo? (President Bill Clinton, Israeli Prime Minister Yitzhak Rabin, and PLO Chairman Yasser Arafat)
2. Look at the map on page 466. How many countries are in the Middle East? (17)
3. Look at the map on page 471. What countries border Israel? (Lebanon, Syria, Jordan, and Egypt)
4. Look at page 474. In 1990, what country did Iran invade? (Kuwait)
5. Look at the timeline on page 479. What five wars are listed? (Israeli-Arab War; Six-Day War; Yom Kippur War; Iran-Iraq War; and Persian Gulf War)

Intermediate Level Questions

Encourage students at this level to offer verbal responses or short written responses to the following questions.

1. Look at the section entitled The State of Israel. How did the United Nations try to resolve the conflict in Palestine? (It divided Palestine in two.)
2. Look at the section entitled Middle East Tensions. Why did the Yom Kippur War occur? (Arab nations were angry because Israel occupied all of the Sinai Peninsula, the Gaza Strip, the West Bank, and East Jerusalem.)
3. Look at the section entitled Oil Power. How is the wealth from oil used in the Middle East? (Much of the profit goes toward building a strong Arab military.)
4. Look at the section entitled Life in the Middle East. Why is Israel one of the most industrialized and advanced nations of the Middle East? (Answers will vary.)
5. Look at the section entitled Life in the Middle East. How is the Middle East today still like the Middle East of ancient civilizations? (Its people continue to fight for land and to be concerned with food production and irrigation, and they argue about religion.)

Advanced Level Questions

Encourage students at this level to provide written responses in complete sentences to the following questions.

1. Why do you think the Arab nations declared war on Israel in 1948? (Answers will vary. Possible answers might include that Arab nations were angered that Israel received land or that the Arab nations saw Israel as a threat.)
2. Why do you think the superpowers became involved in the Arab-Israeli conflict? (Answers will vary. Possible answers might include that tension and conflict in the Middle East has an effect on all countries.)
3. What were the outcomes of the wars that were fought between Israel and Arab nations? (The wars that were fought between Israel and the Arab nations were the Israeli-Arab War, which Israel won, establishing its right as a state; the June 1967, or the Six Days, War, which Israel won, allowing it to occupy the Sinai Peninsula, Gaza Strip, West Bank, and East Jerusalem; and the Yom Kippur War, which Israel won.)
4. Why did the Persian Gulf War occur? (Iraq invaded Kuwait because it wanted to make Kuwait and its rich oil fields a part of Iraq.)
5. Why is OPEC so powerful? (It controls the world's supply of oil.)

Closing the Chapter

Ask students to use the outline they completed for the Organizing Information activity on page 62 of this guide to write a summary about what they learned.

ESL/ELL

Chapter 32: The Death of the Soviet Union

pages 482–495

Introducing the Chapter

Tapping Prior Knowledge
Ask students to preview the chapter by reading the headings and subheadings and by looking at the photos (on pages 482, 485, 489, and 490 of the Student Edition), the map (on page 488 of the Student Edition), and the timeline (on page 493 of the Student Edition). Then, ask students to rewrite each of the Learning Objectives on page 482 of the Student Edition in the form of a question. For example, the first one could be rewritten as What three changes in the Soviet Union was Mikhail Gorbachev responsible for? Ask students, *How can great changes in a powerful country affect the rest of the world?*

Preteaching Vocabulary

Personalizing Vocabulary Begin by asking students to preview the chapter for five unfamiliar words or phrases and to record them in their Word Logs. Once students have identified these words and phrases, ask them to use their dictionaries to define them.

Identifying Essential Vocabulary Go over the pronunciation and meaning of each word and phrase in the box below. Then, distribute the four-column chart on page 80 of this guide. Ask students to work with a partner to find the words and phrases in the box below as they are used in the text. Have the students create a chart using the following headings: **Word or Phrase, Meaning Clues From the Text, Definition** and **My Sentence.**

Word or Phrase	Meaning
hard-line	dealing with something in a very strict way (p.485)
toppled	made something fall over (p.486)
hastened	made something happen faster or sooner (p.486)
woes	problems and troubles (p.487)
ethnic	relating to a particular race, nation, or group and their customs and traditions (p.492)

Applying Content Knowledge

From the Chapter: Learn More About It (page 491)
Ask students to read Learn More About It: The Fall of the Berlin Wall and the Reunification of Germany. Discuss the symbolism of the wall. Ask students, *When people risked their lives to cross the wall to freedom, what kinds of things did they want to be able to do?* Write students' suggestions on the chalkboard. Ask students, *When the Berlin Wall fell, what did that mean for peoples' personal freedom?*

Note-taking
Ask students to read Mikhail Gorbachev Works to Improve Relations on pages 483–484 of the Student Edition and Gorbachev and *Glastnost* on pages 484–485 of the Student Edition. Then, remind students of the difference between a fact and an opinion. Explain to students that a fact is a piece of information that can be measured or proven with evidence, and an opinion is an idea that other people can agree or disagree with. Then, have students find five facts about changes Gorbachev made in the Soviet Union. Ask students to write opinions about each of the facts they listed. Ask students, *Do you agree with what Gorbachev did?*

Using Visuals
Ask students to look at the map entitled Independent Republics on page 488 of the Student Edition and have them list the former Soviet Republics.

Organizing Information
Ask students to create a chart using the following headings: **Satellite Country, Problems with Communism, Revolts and Fighting, Groups Involved, Reasons,** and **Outcome.** Have them list the Soviet satellites and each republic of Yugoslavia discussed on pages 487–493 of the Student Edition under the first column of their chart. You may wish to write the following example on the chalkboard for students to model: *Satellite Country: Hungary; Problems w/Communism: 1956 – tried to cut ties w/Soviets; Revolts and Fighting: Soviet troops entered Hungary; Groups Involved: Soviets & Hungarians; Reasons: Wanted independence; Outcome: Movement was crushed.*

Assessing Content Knowledge

Ask students to respond to the following questions. You may wish to encourage students with higher language proficiency to help beginning level students understand the questions.

Beginning Level Questions

Encourage students at this level to think about the answers to these questions and offer short verbal responses.

1. Look at page 483. What did Mikhail Gorbachev hope to accomplish? (See page 483.)
2. Look at page 486. Who tried to take over the government and remove Gorbachev? (a group of hard-line Communist leaders)
3. Look at page 486. What was the Commonwealth of Independent States? (a loose alliance of 11 states)
4. Look at the map on page 488. How many former Soviet republics are shown? (16)
5. Look at the timeline on page 493. In what year was the Commonwealth of Independent States formed? (in 1991)

Intermediate Level Questions

Encourage students at this level to offer verbal responses or short written responses to the following questions.

1. Look at the sections entitled Mikhail Gorbachev Works to Improve Relations and Gorbachev and *Glastnost*. What were some of the changes that Mikhail Gorbachev made in the Soviet Union? (Answers will vary.)
2. Look at the sections entitled Gorbachev and *Glastnost*. How did *perestroika* affect the economy of the Soviet Union? (See page 485.)
3. Look at the section entitled An Attempted Coup. What was the result of the attempted coup by hard-liners in the Soviet Union? (It hastened the death of communism inside the Soviet Union.)
4. Look at the section entitled The Commonwealth of Independent States. What was the result of the break-up of the Soviet Union? (the creation of 15 independent nations)
5. Look at the section entitled A Wave of Freedom Sweeps Soviet Satellites. How was Lech Walesa affected by the poor economic state of Poland? (He lost his presidency.)

Advanced Level Questions

Encourage students at this level to provide written responses in complete sentences to the following questions.

1. How did military actions by Gorbachev show Soviet influence on other countries? (He pressured Castro to remove troops from Angola and persuaded Vietnam to withdraw from Cambodia.)
2. What problems did *glastnost* cause the Soviet Union? (Many republics wanted their freedom, and violence developed in some areas.)
3. What conclusion(s) can you reach about the result of the Soviets' loosened control over the satellite countries in Eastern Europe in the late 1980s and early 1990s? (Answers may vary. Possible answers might include that violence occurred in many of the countries as different groups pushed for power and freedom; that once controls were lifted, people fought for control; and that some leaders were forced from power and even executed, while others gave in peacefully.)
4. Why do you think communism ended for many countries at the same time? (Answers will vary. Possible answers might include that the countries were geographically close and knew what was happening in the other countries, and since they were all Soviet satellites, they were all affected by *glastnost*, which loosened Soviet control over them.)
5. Why do you think ethnic groups clashed when countries are joined or divided? (Answers will vary.)

Closing the Chapter

Ask students to answer the questions they wrote for the Tapping Prior Knowledge activity on page 64 of this guide. Have students use the answers to their questions to write a summary about what they learned.

ESL/ELL

Chapter 33: Latin America After World War II
pages 496–509

Introducing the Chapter

Tapping Prior Knowledge
Ask students to preview the chapter by reading the headings and subheadings and by looking at the photos (on pages 496, 501, and 503 of the Student Edition), the map (on page 505 of the Student Edition), and the timeline (on page 506 of the Student Edition). Then, direct students to the map on page 505 of the Student Edition. Then, distribute the KWL chart on page 79 of this guide and ask students to complete the K and the W columns of the chart by writing what they know and want to know about Latin America after World War II. Ask students, *What would you like to know about Latin America? How was it affected by World War II?*

Preteaching Vocabulary
Personalizing Vocabulary Begin by asking students to preview the chapter for five unfamiliar words or phrases and to record them in their Word Logs. Once students have identified these words and phrases, ask them to use their dictionaries to define them.

Identifying Essential Vocabulary Go over the pronunciation and meaning of each word and phrase in the box below. Then, ask students to write the sentence where they find the word or phrase in the chapter and then replace it with a word they are familiar with.

Word or Phrase	Meaning
guerrilla	member of an independent fighting group that fights for political reasons and attacks the enemy in small groups (p.498)
pledged	made a promise to give (p.498)
funneled	sent a lot of things or money from different places to one place (p.500)
forbade	told someone not to do something (p.500)
urban	relating to a city (p.504)
civil unrest	fighting between different groups of people in the same country (p.504)
devalue	to reduce the value of money (p.506)

Applying Content Knowledge

From the Chapter: Learn More About It (page 507)
Ask students to read the section entitled Learn More About It: Brazil Pledges to Protect Its Rain Forest on page 507 of the Student Edition. Then, distribute the Who, What, Why, Where, When, and How chart on page 72 of this guide. Have students write **Who benefits from rain forests?** under **Who** in the chart; **What is a rain forest?** under **What** in the chart; **Why are rain forests important?** under **Why** in the chart; **Where are the world's rain forests located?** under **Where** in the chart; **When did Brazil initiate an environmental program to protect the rain forests?** under **When** in the chart; and **How do rain forests affect people's lives?** under **How** in the chart. Have students complete their charts using the information from the text.

Organizing Information
Distribute the Outline on page 76 of this guide. As students read the chapter, ask them to add headings and complete the outline with key details from the chapter. You may wish to ask students to use their completed outlines to write a summary about Latin America after World War II.

Note-taking
Ask students to read Changes in Mexico on page 503 of the Student Edition. Then, ask students to list the causes and effects of Mexico's economic problems. Have students use their lists to write a summary.

Personalizing the Lesson
Ask students, *Why is it important to preserve the world's rain forests?* Ask students to review the Who, What, Why, Where, When, and How chart they created for rain forests from the Chapter activity on page 66 of this guide and work in groups to list ways they can contribute to the preservation of the world's rain forests. You might want to suggest that students research environmental organizations that work to preserve the rain forests. Then, ask students to make a wall-sized class poster that explains and illustrates problems and solutions for the world's rain forests.

ESL/ELL

▶ Assessing Content Knowledge

Ask students to respond to the following questions. You may wish to encourage students with higher language proficiency to help beginning level students understand the questions.

Beginning Level Questions

Encourage students at this level to think about the answers to these questions and offer short verbal responses.

1. Look at page 498. What did Fidel Castro do when he took over Cuba? (set up a Communist dictatorship)
2. Look at page 499. Who fought in the civil war in El Salvador? (rebels and the military government)
3. Look at page 501. Who was Manuel Noriega? (commander of the Panamanian defense forces)
4. Look at page 503. What were two reasons for Mexico's economic crisis in the 1980s? (political corruption and a growing population)
5. Look at the map on page 505. What is the largest South American country that is shown? (Brazil)

Intermediate Level Questions

Encourage students at this level to offer verbal responses or short written responses to the following questions.

1. Look at the section entitled Political Unrest in Central America. What was the effect of the Cuban Revolution on other countries in Latin America? (Communist activity increased.)
2. Look at the section entitled The United States Invades Panama. Why was Manuel Noriega a problem? (He was corrupt and an accused drug smuggler; he tampered with election votes; and he controlled the country.)
3. Look at the section entitled Changes in Mexico. How has NAFTA helped Mexico's economy? (It eased immigration laws, proposed the end of tariffs, and gave trucks free access to border routes.)
4. Look at the section entitled Unrest in Haiti. What are the causes of the problems in Haiti? (revolutions, government takeovers, poverty, drought, hurricanes, and famine)
5. Look at the section entitled Latin America Today. What positive changes had taken place in Latin America by the year 2000? (See page 506.)

Advanced Level Questions

Encourage students at this level to provide written responses in complete sentences to the following questions.

1. What were the effects of Castro's takeover in Cuba, and how did that takeover affect its relationship with the United States? (Cuba became a Communist country, and the United States and Cuba became unfriendly.)
2. Why did the United States support the Contras and some military dictators in Latin America? (The United States feared that Latin America might become Communist.)
3. Was the United States justified in selling arms to Iran to raise money to fund the Contras? Explain your answer. (Answers will vary. Accept all reasonable responses.)
4. Was the United States justified in sending troops to Panama? (Answers will vary. Accept all reasonable responses.)
5. Do you think the United States should have returned the people to Haiti who tried to enter the United States illegally? (Answers will vary. Accept all reasonable responses.)

▶ Closing the Chapter

Ask students to complete the L column of the KWL charts that they began for the Tapping Prior Knowledge activity on page 66 of this guide. Then, have them use their completed KWL charts to write a summary about what they learned.

Chapter 34: The World Today

pages 510–525

Introducing the Chapter

Tapping Prior Knowledge

Ask students to preview the chapter by reading the headings and subheadings and by looking at the photos (on pages 510, 513, 515, 517, and 522 of the Student Edition) and the timeline (on page 523 of the Student Edition). Then ask students to look at the heading The Shrinking World on page 517 of the Student Edition. Ask students, *Why is the world shrinking?* Students should recognize that technology has made the world seem smaller. Ask students, *Can our shrinking world become a peaceful place, or will it continue to be a world filled with conflict and danger?* Encourage students to share their opinions and feelings. Write their opinions and feelings on the chalkboard. Ask students, *What kinds of issues do you think the world will continue to have to deal with in the coming years?*

Preteaching Vocabulary

Personalizing Vocabulary Begin by asking students to preview the chapter for five unfamiliar words or phrases and to record them in their Word Logs. Once students have identified these words and phrases, ask them to use their dictionaries to define them.

Identifying Essential Vocabulary Go over the pronunciation and meaning of each word in the box below. Then, distribute the four-column chart on page 80 of this guide. Ask students to create a chart with the headings: **Word, Sentence From the Text, Synonym,** and **My Sentence**. To find synonyms for each word, ask students to use their bilingual dictionaries and context clues from the Student Edition.

Word	Meaning
nuclear	using the atomic nucleus, atomic energy, or the atom bomb (p.511)
age	period of time associated with a special person or thing (p.511)
energy	the resources for power (p.512)
communications	system of sending messages (p.518)

Applying Content Knowledge

From the Chapter: Learn More About It (page 516)

Ask students to read Learn More About It: The Computer Age on page 516 of the Student Edition. Then, ask students to work in groups to create a list of the positive and negative aspects of computers. Have students use their lists to write a summary about the positive and negative aspects of computers. Ask students, *How have computers changed our lives for the better? For the worse? How might we be using computers ten years from now?*

Using Visuals

Ask students to look at the photo on page 522 of the Student Edition. Ask students to recall what they learned about the Olympics on page 97 of the Student Edition. Then, ask students, *Why do so many countries want to host the Olympics?* Students' answers may include the desire to showcase their country to the rest of the world, the pride of being chosen as a host city, and the economic advantage of having thousands of people visit their city. Then, ask students to work in small groups to choose a country to host the next Olympics. Ask students, *Why did you choose the country you chose?* Then, have students suggest a design for the medals that would be given to the winners. You may wish to have students illustrate their design concepts.

Note-taking

Distribute the Spider Web on page 73 of this guide. Ask students to write *The World Today* in the central shape and label the spokes of the web **Energy, Space Exploration, Economy,** and **Women's Roles**. As students read the chapter, ask them to complete their webs using key details from the chapter. Then, distribute index cards and ask students to work in pairs and use their webs to write one question about energy, one question about space exploration, one question about the economy, and one question about women's roles. You may wish to collect all the cards and ask the whole class one question and engage students in a debate, or you may wish to ask pairs of students to trade questions with each other.

ESL/ELL

▶ Assessing Content Knowledge

Ask students to respond to the following questions. You may wish to encourage students with higher language proficiency to help beginning level students understand the questions.

Beginning Level Questions

Encourage students at this level to think about the answers to these questions and offer short verbal responses.

1. Look at pages 512–513. What can happen when there is an accident at a nuclear power plant? (contamination; radiation; evacuation of people; and death)
2. Look at page 515. What happened to the space shuttle *Challenger*? (It exploded shortly after takeoff.)
3. Look at page 517. What developments have made the world seem smaller? (developments in transportation and communication)
4. Look at page 518. What does the term *Pacific Rim* describe? (the lands bordering the Pacific Ocean)
5. Look at the timeline on page 523. When did man first walk on the moon? (in 1969)

Intermediate Level Questions

Encourage students at this level to offer verbal responses or short written responses to the following questions.

1. Look at the section entitled The Nuclear Age. How did the idea of nuclear power first begin? (Einstein said that energy was contained in every atom.)
2. Look at the section entitled The Space Age. How has space travel changed since 1957? (It changed from unmanned satellites to one-man flights to having many on the space shuttle.)
3. Look at the section entitled The Space Age. How is space being explored today? (unmanned spaceships, multinational cooperation on the ISS, and space shuttle flights.)
4. Look at the section entitled A Global Economy. What is the goal of the European Union? (to ensure free trade and free movement between member nations)
5. Look at the section entitled Developed Nations and Developing Nations. Why are developing countries more dependent on other nations? (The economies in developing countries can be easily upset.)

Advanced Level Questions

Encourage students at this level to provide written responses in complete sentences to the following questions.

1. Do you believe that space exploration is important? Explain your answer. (Answers will vary. Accept all reasonable responses.)
2. Why do you think it is important for people to live on the International Space Station? (Answers will vary. Possible answers might include that living in space allows you to learn more about it in a shorter period of time.)
3. Are there disadvantages to a shrinking world? Explain your answer. (Answers will vary. Accept all reasonable responses.)
4. How do multinational companies help the world economy? (Each nation depends on the other for financial success.)
5. Why does it seem as if history has repeated itself throughout the course of time? Explain your answer. (Answers will vary. Accept all reasonable responses.)

▶ Closing the Chapter

Ask students to rewrite each heading in the chapter in the form of a question. For example, the section entitled The Nuclear Age could be rewritten as What is the Nuclear Age? and the section entitled Peaceful Uses of Nuclear Energy could be rewritten as What are some peaceful uses of nuclear energy? or How can people make sure that nuclear energy is used for peaceful purposes? Once students have rewritten each heading in the form of a question, have students write answers for each of the questions.

About the Graphic Organizers

Graphic organizers are valuable tools for ESL/ELL students. They show patterns and relationships that support language acquisition and that help students access academic content, consolidate their thinking, and help them to generate new ideas. For example, the Who, What, Why, Where, When, and How chart gives students an opportunity to use adverbs to write *wh-* questions as a method for accessing content.

The graphic organizers and visuals provided here can be used in a variety of ways. They can be made into overhead slides and used for visual instruction or for group work. The pages can also be reproduced for use by students. All of the graphic organizers correlate to an activity in this guide. Students can use them to complete their activities, adding to them as needed. Below is a description of each graphic organizer and visual with suggestions for their use. Each of these graphic organizers can also be downloaded from www.esl-ell.com.

Who, What, Why, Where, When, and How Chart (page 72)
This graphic organizer is used to help students identify important information while they read. Students complete the chart by answering the questions as they read. This chart can be used to help students understand news articles they may read.

Spider Web (page 73)
This graphic organizer is used to organize several levels of elaboration. The main topic is written in the center circle. Attributes are listed on the spokes. Specific details are listed on the horizontal lines extending from each spoke. This organizer can also be used to determine main ideas and supporting details. You may also want students to use a Spider Web when brainstorming ideas.

Venn Diagram (page 74)
This graphic organizer is used to compare and contrast things or ideas. Each circle should be labeled as one of the two things being contrasted. Then, the differences are written in the outer section of each circle. The similarities are written in the section in which the circles overlap.

Timeline (page 75)
This graphic organizer is used to organize a series of events.

Outline (page 76)
This graphic organizer is used to help students organize and write outlines. An outline can be used to organize fully developed ideas into paragraphs in which supporting details are given. For activities that require longer outlines, outlines can be extended by continuing the numbering on the back of the reproducible page.

Sequence of Events Chart (page 77)
This graphic organizer is a flowchart to help students sort information chronologically. You may wish to have students use this graphic organizer when making to-do lists and writing out directions. Students might also use the Sequence of Events chart to plan out role-playing activities or while writing conversations.

Description Web (page 78)
This graphic organizer is used to cluster supporting details around a central topic. It is very useful for brainstorming. The main concept or idea is written in the center shape. Related ideas are listed in the outer shapes.

KWL Chart (page 79)
This chart can be used before and after each chapter in the Student Edition. The KWL chart is used to help students access their knowledge of a topic and to add to what they already know. KWL stands for "Know," "Want To Know," and "Learned."

Four-column Chart (page 80)
This graphic organizer can be used for many purposes. The columns can be labeled as needed. Then, relevant information is written in each cell of the chart.

Idea Web (page 81)
This graphic organizer is used to cluster supporting details around a central topic. It is very useful for brainstorming. The main concept or idea is written in the center shape. Related ideas are listed in the outer shapes.

Individual Activity Rubric (page 82)
The Individual Activity Rubric can be customized for different activities. The first eight criteria in the rubric are generic. The last two criteria are left blank. These criteria should be based on specific tasks required and filled in by the teacher. You may wish to distribute a rubric to students as a guide for completing an activity or as a self-assessment tool.

Group Activity Rubric (page 83)
The Group Activity Rubric can be customized for different activities. The first eight criteria in the rubric are generic. The last two criteria are left blank. These criteria should be based on specific tasks required and filled in by the teacher. You may wish to distribute a rubric to students as a guide for completing a group activity or as a self-assessment tool for a student who worked in a group.

Chapter Goals and Self-assessment (page 84)
This reproducible can be used for goal-setting and self-assessment. When starting a chapter, have students write the Chapter Learning Objectives onto this worksheet. At the end of the chapter, students can self-check their understanding by writing about it. They can also record the date when they completed all of their objectives.

Name _____ Date _____

Who, What, Why, Where, When, and How Chart

WHO	
WHAT	
WHY	
WHERE	
WHEN	
HOW	

Name _____ Date _____

Spider Web

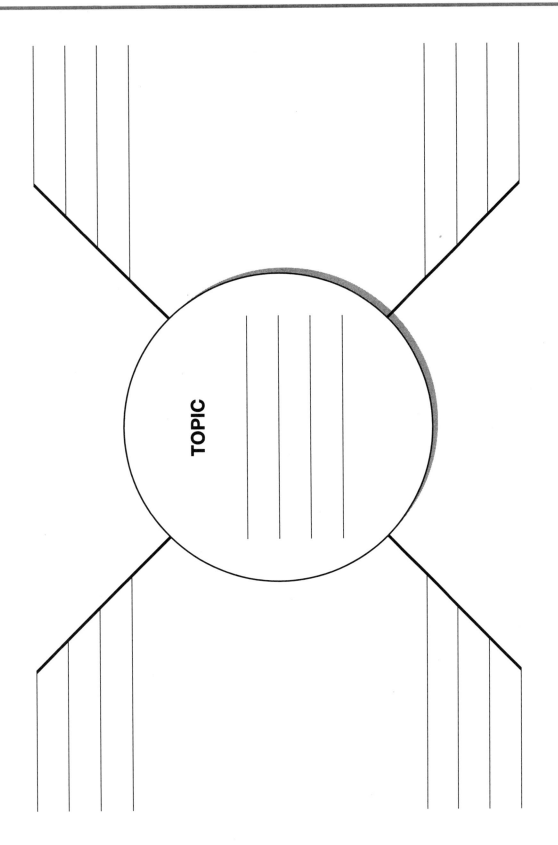

Graphic Organizers • 73

Name _____ Date _____

Venn Diagram

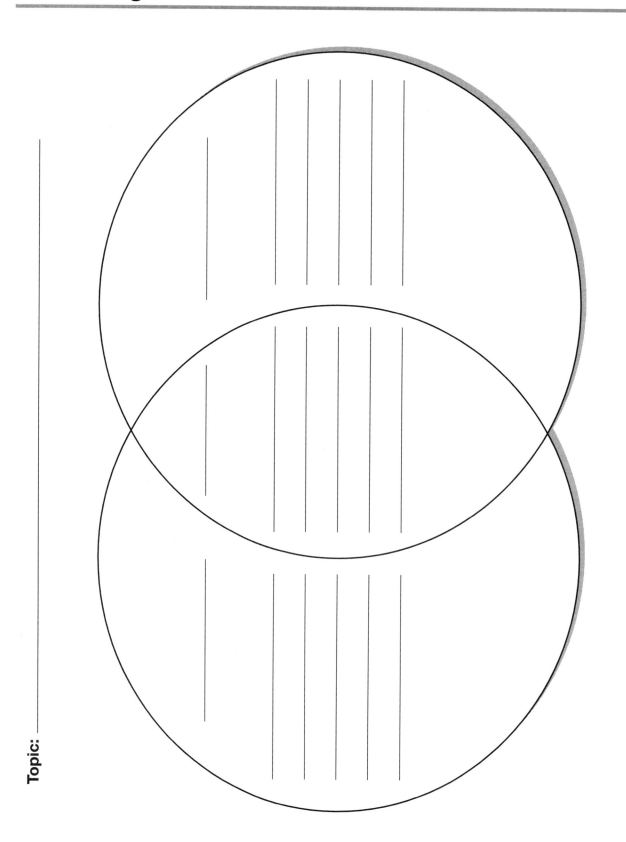

Topic: _____

Name _____ Date _____

Timeline

ESL/ELL

Name _____ Date _____

Outline

Topic: _____

I. _____

    A. _____

        1. _____

        2. _____

    B. _____

        1. _____

        2. _____

    C. _____

        1. _____

        2. _____

II. _____

    A. _____

        1. _____

        2. _____

    B. _____

        1. _____

        2. _____

    C. _____

        1. _____

        2. _____

Name _____ Date _____

Sequence of Events Chart

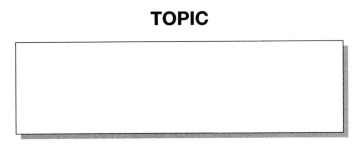

TOPIC

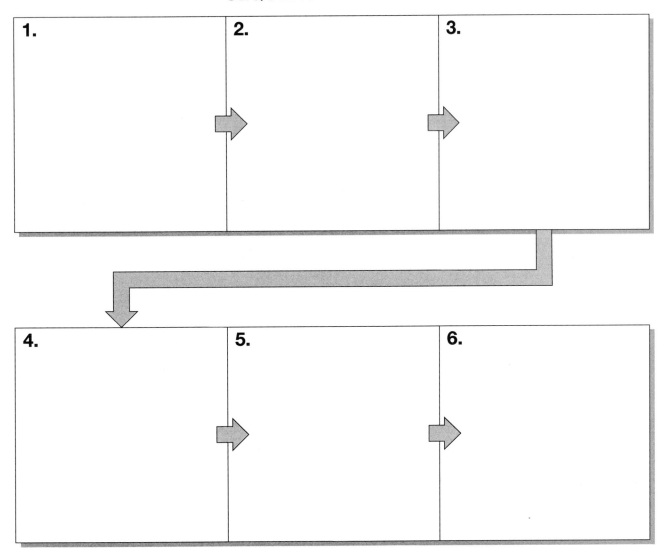

SEQUENCE OF EVENTS

1.
2.
3.
4.
5.
6.

Graphic Organizers • 77

Name _____ Date _____

Description Web

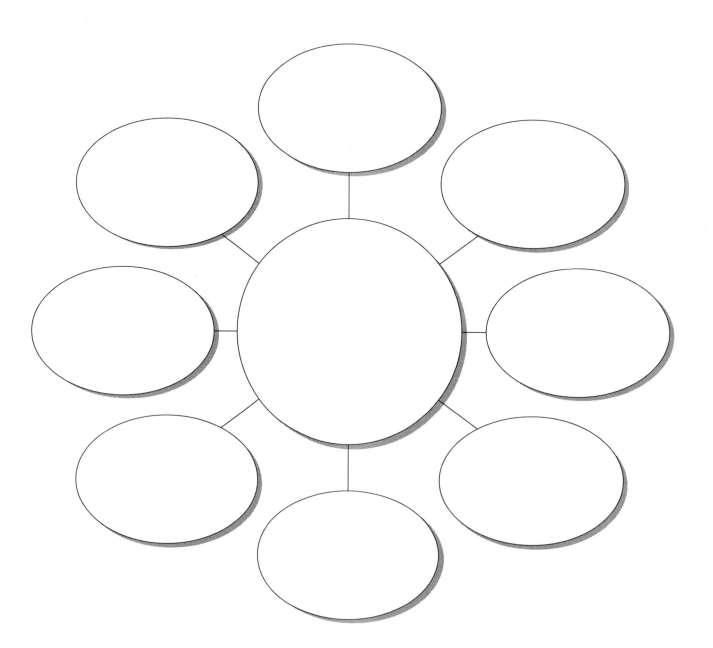

Name _____ Date _____

KWL Chart

K (What I Know)	W (What I Want to Know)	L (What I Have Learned)

ESL/ELL

Name _____ Date _____

Four-column Chart

Topic: _____

Name _____ Date _____

Idea Web

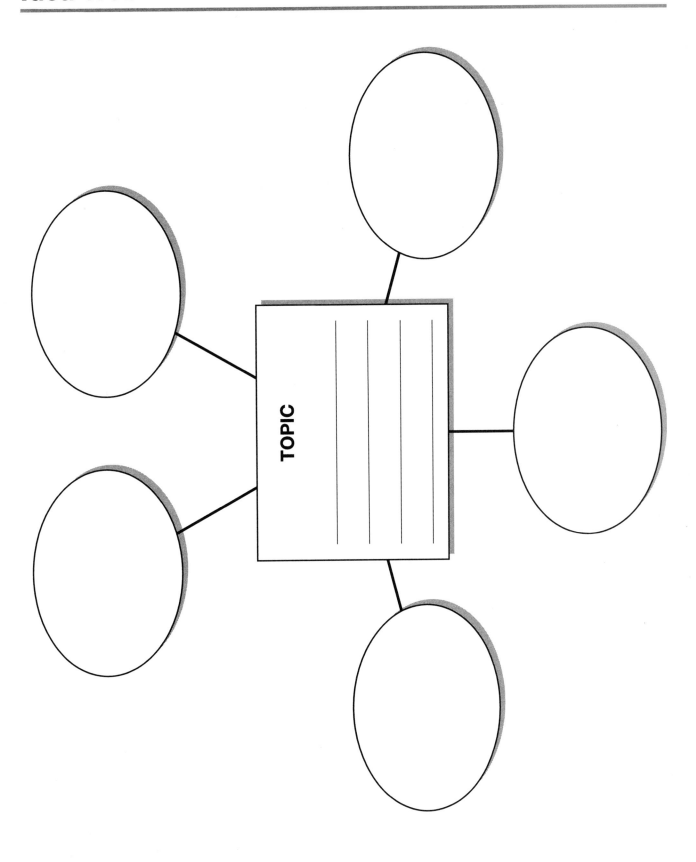

Individual Activity Rubric

Name _____ Date _____

Chapter Number _____ Activity _____

Directions
Check ✓ one box in a column to finish each sentence.
Give each check ✓ the assigned number of points.
Add the points in each column. Write the sum. Then add across to find the total score.
You may wish to add two criteria of your own to the rubric.

	POINTS	**10**	**9**	**8**	**7**	**6**
For this activity, Student's name _____		all of the time	most of the time	half of the time	less than half of the time	none of the time
followed directions						
asked questions when help was needed						
worked independently when required						
used appropriate resources and materials						
completed assigned tasks						
showed an understanding of the content						
presented materials without errors						
explained thinking with support						
_____						
_____						
	POINTS	+	+	+	+	=

TOTAL SCORE

82 • Graphic Organizers

Group Activity Rubric

Name _____ Date _____

Chapter Number _____ Activity _____

Directions
Check ✓ one box in a column to finish each sentence.
Give each check ✓ the assigned number of points.
Add the points in each column. Write the sum. Then add across to find the total score.
You may wish to add two criteria of your own to the rubric.

For this activity, Student's name _____	POINTS	10 all of the time	9 most of the time	8 half of the time	7 less than half of the time	6 none of the time
followed directions						
asked questions when help was needed						
worked independently when required						
used appropriate resources and materials						
completed assigned tasks						
showed an understanding of the content						
presented materials without errors						
explained thinking with support						
_____						
_____						
	POINTS	+	+	+	+	=

TOTAL SCORE

Graphic Organizers • 83

ESL/ELL

Chapter Goals and Self-assessment

Name _____ Date _____

Chapter Title _____ Pages _____

Write each Learning Objective on a line below.

Did I understand it?

Yes   No

- _____   ❏   ❏

- _____   ❏   ❏

- _____   ❏   ❏

- _____   ❏   ❏

- _____   ❏   ❏

- _____   ❏   ❏

Complete each statement.

This chapter is about _____

_____

An important history fact, person, or event from this chapter is _____

_____

I learned a writing skill. It is _____

_____

I completed Chapter _____ entitled _____

_____ and all of my Learning Objectives on

_____ .